BEDSIDE BOOK OF
BAD GIRLS

OUTLAW WOMEN OF THE AMERICAN WEST

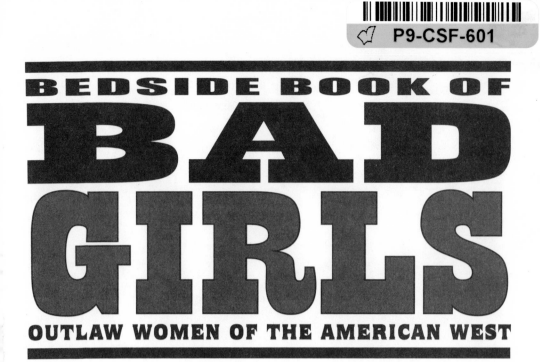

BY MICHAEL RUTTER

FARCOUNTRY
PRESS

HELENA, MONTANA

ISBN 10: 1-56037-462-4
ISBN 13: 978-1-56037-462-6

© 2008 by Farcountry Press
Text © 2008 by Michael Rutter

For more information on our books, write Farcountry Press, P.O. Box 5630, Helena, MT 59604; call (800) 821-3874; or visit www.farcountrypress.com.

Library of Congress Cataloging-in-Publication Data

Rutter, Michael, 1953-
  Bedside book of bad girls : outlaw women of the American West / by Michael Rutter.
     p. cm.
  ISBN-13: 978-1-56037-462-6
  ISBN-10: 1-56037-462-4
1. Women outlaws--West (U.S.)--Biography. 2. Women outlaws--West (U.S.)--History.
3. Outlaws--West (U.S.)--Biography. 4. Outlaws--West (U.S.)--History. 5. West (U.S.)--Biography.
6. Frontier and pioneer life--West (U.S.) I. Title.
  F590.5.R86 2008
  364.3092'2--dc22
  [B]
                                        2007033332

Created, produced, and designed in the United States.
Printed in the Canada.

13   12   11   10   09   08   1   2   3   4   5   6

TABLE OF CONTENTS

ACKNOWLEDGMENTS

My special thanks to the Deadwood Historical Preservation Commission. Your help has been invaluable with this project.

I'd also like to thank the Orem, Utah, Public Library.

INTRODUCTION

On the western frontier, resilient men and women hacked a daunting life out of an expansive wilderness. Because of the physical demands of life in the West—women worked alongside men on the homesteads—western women were not as indentured to societal conventions and traditional norms as those in the East. There was little time for fancy tea parties or parlor socials. They shot mule deer to feed the family, killed rattlesnakes in the barn, hoed corn in the July sun, and mucked out the stalls. If needed, they would perform physical labor with the men, as well as do the cooking, the cleaning, and the child rearing. They ran the ranch or farm when their husbands were away on cattle drives, getting supplies, or locating strays.

Western women achieved a greater measure of political independence than their more genteel sisters in the East—they were among the first to vote, serve in public office, and hold official appointments.

Many western women were as adept at living off the land as their male counterparts. A frontier woman was often skilled in the use of so-called men's tools, including firearms, which were essential for survival in the West. Many western women could use a rifle to some extent, and nearly all could point and fire the family scatter gun with deadly, albeit short-range, effect. A number could also use pistols. Most western women could saddle and bridle a horse or hitch up a team. In a large land with untold miles between spreads and towns, equestrian abilities were not a Sunday hobby; they were critical survival skills.

When a western woman committed a crime, it caused a media frenzy. Eastern audiences were fascinated with the western frontier; add a gun-totin' female to the mix, and it was a hot story indeed. Journalists needed to sell their copy. If the facts didn't have enough punch, writers got creative and livened them up. For a journalist, the sin wasn't stretching the truth; the sin was telling a flat tale.

Ask people today to name the most famous outlaws in the West and they'll most likely mention Billy the Kid, Jesse James, and Butch Cassidy, among others. In addition to these outlaws, however, two other names almost always appear on the list—Calamity Jane and Belle Starr.

Darlings of the eastern press, Calamity Jane and Belle Starr were two of the most infamous villains in the American West. Their deeds, however, were greatly exaggerated in order to sell papers. The two women were not superheroes, nor the gun-slinging female outlaws portrayed in newspapers, dime novels, and pulp fiction of the day. In reality, Belle Starr was little more than a horse thief. Calamity Jane was an alcoholic vagabond who resorted to prostitution and petty theft to survive.

Several female outlaws perpetrated particularly vicious crimes. Kate Bender and Ma Steffleback were some of the bloodiest serial killers in American history. Kate Bender slit the throats of her victims after bashing their brains in with a sledgehammer; Ma Steffleback reportedly watched her accomplices smash the heads of their drunken victims with the back of an ax, then picked the dead folks' pockets and dumped their bodies in abandoned mine shafts.

Elizabeth Potts, the first woman hanged in Nevada, participated in a grisly murder with her husband; under her direction, he murdered a man, chopped up his body, and tried to burn the remains before burying them.

Madam Moustache was considered one of the best gamblers in the West until the drink got to her. She is said to have murdered one of her husbands after he stole everything she had worked for—and she was suspected of killing another man, too.

Ah Toy, the brutal Chinese madam, abducted Chinese girls and sold them to brothels in California during the Gold Rush.

Sally Skull ran guns during the Civil War and was alleged to have killed two of her five husbands.

Although not as well known, several other women displayed a passion for the criminal life. Madam Vestal was a partner in the infamous Deadwood Stage robberies. Pearl Hart and Cora Hubbard were armed robbers; Hart held up a stage, and Hubbard participated in a bank robbery. Elizabeth Bassett, her daughters Josie and Ann, and Ellen Watson were not so much criminals as targets for big-time ranchers who falsely accused them of being rustlers in order to drive them off their land.

Little Britches and Cattle Annie were just teenagers when they started stealing. Their crimes made the front page because they were female, and because newspapers sensationalized their misdeeds. As soon as they were released from prison, they were all but forgotten.

Some of the women were labeled as outlaws because of their associations with notorious men. The members of the Wild Bunch were some of the most wanted felons in the country. The women who kept company with them were guilty by association, or sometimes were accessories. After a heist, these female companions were always eager to help spend the outlaws' ill-gotten gain, and all participated in money laundering. A few even strapped on six-guns and participated in robberies. Etta Place, Annie Rogers, and Laura Bullion had prices on their heads for participation in large-scale thefts. Two of the women did hard jail time. The Rose of Cimarron, aka Rose Dunn, committed no crimes at all. The story of her outlaw exploits, complete with an invented love interest with a Doolin Gang member, was embroidered to entertain eastern readers.

Indeed, much of frontier folklore is based on tall tales and sensationalism. That's not something we always need to apologize for. Mythology and folklore are part of our cultural literary heritage, after all, and can teach us about ourselves. But along with the wild-west hyperbole, we also need the truth—which is often more fascinating than fiction. The women in this book were genuine people; they lived real lives, faced genuine problems, and made bad choices. They also helped shape the American West. ⊷

SERIAL KILLERS

HARPIES
MOST
HORRIBLE

KATE BENDER AND MA STEFFLEBACK WERE TWO cold-blooded murderesses who stopped at nothing to get what they wanted. Historical accounts vary, but between these two gory killers at least twenty were slain at their hands.

Kate Bender killed because she apparently liked it. Her slayings were almost ceremonial: She wielded her razor-sharp knife and slit throats like a skilled surgeon. Like her partners in crime—known as the Bloody Benders—she didn't seem to care if her victims were adults or children. And some of her victims are believed to have been buried alive. The *Kansas City Times* suggested in 1873, "Nothing like this sickening series of crimes had ever been recorded in the whole history of the country."

Ma Steffleback killed for expediency; a dead man told no tales. While only a few of her victims' bodies were recovered, there was enough evidence to put her in prison until she died in 1909. Criminal investigations at the time weren't sophisticated enough to provide a reliable tally. How many corpses she dumped down abandoned mine shafts, we'll never know. ⊷

CHAPTER ONE

KATE BENDER

The Benders' Bloody Inn

Dr. William York reined his horse toward the Bender Inn. It had been a long day on the Osage Road, and he was tired and hungry. He didn't think he could make it another five miles to the small town of Cherryvale. In retrospect, he should have pushed on in spite of his fatigue.

The doctor was traveling a lonely section of southeastern Kansas between Fort Scott and his home in Independence. Although little more than a cabin, the Bender Inn was a welcome sight. York hardly noticed the crudely painted sign that read GROCERIES above the rough-hewn door. Besides a meal, he knew he could get a bed for the night and a bit of grain for his horse.

Labette County, Kansas, in 1873 was still a dangerous place for a solitary man to travel. Osage Indian raids and outlaw attacks were not uncommon in this section of wild country. Besides visiting his brother in Fort Smith, York had also come looking for clues about a good friend and his daughter who had gone missing several months earlier. They were believed to have traveled this route.

At the inn, York didn't pay much attention to Ma or Pa Bender, who seemed unsociable and standoffish. Their son, Junior, appeared nice enough, although perhaps a simpleton. The doctor did, however, feast his eyes upon the hostess, the twenty-three-year-old Kate Bender. Her auburn hair and trim figure were a refreshing sight after a long day on the trail. Kate was not only pretty, she was also a charming conversationalist. Locally, she was known as a psychic, occasionally holding séances and lectures on spiritualism. The comely woman welcomed the travel-worn York into the inn, where a canvas screen separated the eating area from the kitchen and the sleeping cots.

Kate seated her guest with his back to the curtain and fed the hungry man while she talked to him about spiritualism and dazzled him with food, drink, and conversation. Perhaps she talked of free love, one of her tenets. At some point after the dinner, York leaned his head back against the canvas divider. Waiting behind the screen, Pa and Junior sprang into action, bashing the doctor's skull with a pair of heavy mallets. If the blows weren't enough to kill the doctor, Kate took care of that. She rushed forward with her knife and coldly slit York's throat from ear to ear. Next, she expertly rifled through York's pockets for anything of value. Within minutes, the blood was mopped up, the booty stashed, and the body unceremoniously dropped into the kitchen cellar. The Bloody Benders, as this infamous quartet of serial killers would later be called, had just bagged another victim.

The Benders would be known in history as some of the most nefarious mass murderers in the West. From 1872 to 1873, they operated out of what locals would later call "the Benders' Bloody Inn." Historians have never learned exactly how many victims (including children) met the mallet and knife at their malevolent hands. The bodies—and body parts—of at least twenty people were found on the Benders' property. Some have suggested the number of victims could be as high as forty.

The story of the Bender Inn has its roots in the post–Civil War period. Settlers complained that the Osage Indians, who had been given a portion of southeastern Kansas by treaty, should be moved so that whites could use the tribal land "the way God intended." Among the first wave of settlers was a cult of spiritualists who took up residence near the

Osage Trail (later called the Osage Road). The town of Cherryvale sprang up a few miles away. Among this group of cultists were John Bender and his son, John, Jr., and each settled a section of good prairie land. The Bender women arrived after the men had made the place habitable.

The spiritualists were strange, but they were industrious. They came to Sunday meetings and were deemed innocuous enough. After a while, two of the five families could not take prairie life and moved back to more settled areas. The Benders, though, seemed to prosper. They had an enviable garden and an excellent orchard with more than fifty trees. To help make ends meet, they also opened up an inn and grocery store for the travelers along the road. They offered meals, beds for the night, and a livery with grain for livestock. In the store they sold ammunition, powder and lead balls, canned goods, dried fruit, jerked meat, and tobacco, among other incidentals. It was said that if the inn had no guests in the evening, one could see the Benders out working in their beloved orchard. The ground around the trees was frequently harrowed and exceptionally well groomed.

John "Pa" Bender, the neighbors commented, was sometimes hard to understand, because of his German accent. He was thought to be in his late fifties. A large man for his day—at more than six feet tall—with black caterpillar eyebrows, he mostly kept to himself. His son, John, Jr., was a reasonably good-looking man in his twenties who was known to talk to himself as he walked or worked, and he was thought to be a little slow. But, like his father, he was a hard worker, and in those times hard work covered a multitude of sins.

Kate Bender was the only one of the four who was considered outgoing. She was affable and friendly, the sort of woman who was instantly liked by everyone. Still, she had ruffled the community with her revolutionary philosophies. She was considered by some at the time to be Satanic ("free love" in Christian small-town Kansas in the 1870s was a bit too avant-garde). But while her ideas offended some of the locals, her reputation as a looker, a hostess, and a psychic drew a number of interested customers. So did her hazel eyes and well-proportioned figure.

On occasion, Kate took her presentation on the road, visiting towns around Kansas. She was sometimes billed at lectures as a "Professor of

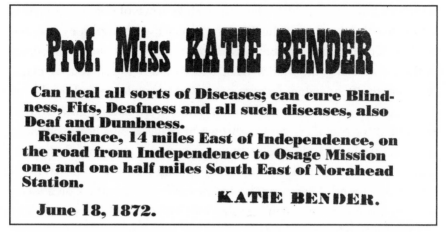

Prof. Miss KATIE BENDER

Can heal all sorts of Diseases; can cure Blindness, Fits, Deafness and all such diseases, also Deaf and Dumbness.
Residence, 14 miles East of Independence, on the road from Independence to Osage Mission one and one half miles South East of Norahead Station.

KATIE BENDER.

June 18, 1872.

Kate Bender used advertisements such as this one to promote her business. Calling herself a "professor," she traveled around Kansas to lecture to groups about psychic phenomenon and spiritual healing. KANSAS STATE HISTORICAL SOCIETY, TOPEKA.

the Supernatural." People who were interested in psychic phenomenon or who needed spiritual healing were said to seek her out. She professed to have the gift of "second sight," the ability to see into the future. She said she could communicate with spirits and could heal with herbs and charms. Kate was the perfect front woman for a confidence game.

Ma Bender also claimed to be a psychic medium, although it was said she wasn't as good as her daughter. A large woman in her early fifties, Ma was said to have a temper, and she kept her husband and son in line. She never seemed to be angry at Kate, however.

It doesn't appear that the other families in the spiritualist group knew anything about the extracurricular activities at the Bender Inn. And the family members, with Kate as the ringleader, took good care to cover their tracks.

The Benders largely targeted lonely souls who wouldn't be readily missed. After they were satisfied that the man was a good prospect, they would kill him and rob him. Travelers usually were safe from Bender malice if they were in a group or if there was another guest present. If a traveler had a local connection, if someone knew he was staying at the Bender Inn, or if the person was a regular, he would also be safe. Cattle buyers, investors, land speculators, and travelers did business cash-on-thebarrelhead, making it difficult to trace their whereabouts—and making them ideal Bender marks. The Benders preferred victims on long sojourns. Such a person might not be missed for months, and the likelihood of authorities tracing the victim back to the southeastern Kansas plains, let alone the Bender Inn, were remote. Besides, violence and trouble on the Osage Road were not uncommon. There were natural hazards to be accounted for, including getting thrown or dragged by a horse, bitten by a snake, caught in a blizzard or tornado, or swept away in a flash flood, among other things. Folks simply vanished, and sometimes their remains were never found. There was also the possibility of an attack on a lonely stretch. More than one man was shot and killed for his horse or saddle, not to mention his poke of cash.

By 1873, however, the number of disappearances along the Osage Road had gotten so high that officials and local residents began paying attention. This region in southeastern Kansas had become one of the most dangerous places to travel in the West.

The proverbial pot came to a boil with the disappearance of William York in the spring of 1873. When the doctor didn't return, his wife and brothers (including one who lived in Independence and another, Colonel A. M. York, who lived in Fort Scott) used their considerable political influence to initiate an investigation.

Oddly enough, it was partly William York's own investigation that had drawn him down the road in the first place in March of 1873. In December of 1872 York's friend, George Loncher, had taken his seven-year-old daughter to visit relatives in Iowa while he sorted out his life after the death of his beloved wife. Loncher and his child never reached their destination and seemed to have vanished without a trace. York wanted to retrace their route and find out what had happened to them.

When William York himself vanished, his brother, Colonel York, personally led an investigation in early May of 1873 to find him. It didn't take long before he concluded that Cherryvale, near the Bender Inn, was the best place to begin.

It was common knowledge that the doctor had stopped at the Bender Inn for an early meal, then, according to the Benders, had continued on his way. The Benders were apparently the last people to see him alive.

Cherryvale residents, eager to help in any way they could, cooperated whole-heartedly with Colonel York. At a town meeting—attended by Pa Bender—most of the locals pledged to support the investigation. Nearly all the homesteaders were honest folk who were also worried about the dangers of the Osage Road—a road they, themselves, had to travel from time to time. Volunteers stepped forward to join a search party, which soon boasted more than fifty men. According to some accounts, even Kate Bender joined the effort, promising to consult the spirits to see if they could help find the missing man.

Colonel York and his party divided up to better search the area. By the time York and his men reached the Bender Inn, the Benders were gone. It appeared the family had not fled quickly but rather had taken the time to pack the items they wanted to bring with them.

Colonel York led a search of the deserted Bender home. What he and the others found was horrific. Finding the kitchen cellar nailed shut, the men pried the nails loose and opened the door. A horrible smell overtook them. Inside the cellar were globs of dried blood everywhere, and blood-soaked earth. The gore from eighteen months of gruesome work had made the cellar stench the stuff of nightmares.

York thought there might be bodies buried under the cabin floor. Expecting the worst, the men ripped up the floor to search for victims, literally taking the cabin apart piece by piece. The men spread out to search the entire property. In the orchard they noticed depressions in the ground and places where the soil was soft. They dug down and found human feet not far from the surface. Digging farther, they found the man that Colonel York had been looking for; his brother William was buried head first. They also found the bodies of William York's good friend, George Loncher, and his young daughter.

Consider the following report about the girl's condition in the *Kansas City Journal*, published in the summer of 1873, not long after the murders were discovered: "[She] was probably eight years of age and had long sunny hair. One arm was broken. The right knee had been wrenched from its socket and the leg doubled up under her body. Nothing like this sickening series of crimes had ever been recorded in the history of the country."

After bodies were discovered at the Bender farm and orchard in 1873, the property became a gruesome tourist attraction. The curious came from near and far to walk around the grave mounds and ponder the grisly murders. Visitors would sometimes take pieces of the cabin or other items as souvenirs of their visit to the Bender Inn.
KANSAS STATE HISTORICAL SOCIETY, TOPEKA.

It is little wonder that the Bender farm was dubbed "Hell's Acre" by the searchers who dug up the bodies. No man in his wildest imagination had expected anything so atrocious or revolting.

Some men used gate rods from the wagons to assist in searching for bodies. In places where the rod was easily pushed into the ground, they suspected a grave and often found a corpse.

After examining clothing and other personal effects, the searchers were able to positively identify seven bodies. Others were simply unrecognizable. In some graves they simply found dismembered body parts. Besides the Loncher girl, there was at least one other child. There was evidence that the Benders had buried one or more of the children alive.

As quickly as it was determined that the Benders were the murderers, the nineteenth-century version of an all-points bulletin went out for them; but the villains had a head start. Searchers at first were able to follow their wagon tracks. But the Bender family eventually caught a train and split up before the telegraph could disseminate the message for officials to apprehend them.

According to one account, a posse actually nabbed them and in righteous indignation savagely shot Ma, Pa, and Junior, then buried Kate upside down and alive.

We can safely assume that such a story, as much as it inspires a sense of justice, is just that—a story. While we can understand the possibility of such an event, the men surely would have brought the bodies back to Cherryvale had it really happened. They would have been local heroes. Besides, there was a considerable reward for the Benders—the governor of Kansas offered $2,000, Colonel York offered $1,000—and the posse would have wanted to cash in.

In the end, reporters and lawmen discovered that Ma Bender was really a confidence woman named Almira Meil Griffin, from New York. It's alleged, too, that she may have murdered a few of her former husbands. Her daughter Kate, it turned out, was Eliza Griffin. She, too, was a gifted confidence woman and thief involved in séances and supernatural scams. It is possible that she also dabbled in prostitution. Pa's real name was John Flickinger, and he was a native of Germany. He may have been married to Ma at one time, or perhaps he was just her partner in crime. Junior was a man named John Gebhardt, who may have been living with Kate (some feel they were married) at the inn.

When the band split up with the law on their heels, Ma and Pa went their separate ways. It was thought that Kate and Junior took off together. Rumors of Bender "sightings" occurred for a decade, but no trace of their whereabouts was ever discovered.

For all their homicidal activities, the "Bloody Benders" were thought to have netted about $5,000 in cash and gold, along with saddles, horses, wagons and teams, and other items. The search for the murderers was intense, but there were few leads. Kate and the other Benders escaped their earthly judges. ⊷

CHAPTER TWO

MA STEFFLEBACK
Galena's Bloody Madam

⟜⟞———⟝⟞

Ma Steffleback had a voracious appetite for money. She was a ruthless woman who would kill for pocket change. It wasn't enough that she served cheap whiskey and willing girls to the local miners (and whoever else was interested), or that she knew how to rig a game of chance. Fortunes were being made overnight, and she wanted a substantial slice.

Steffleback had a lucrative two-story brothel—a type of gold mine in itself—in Galena, Kansas, but its profits weren't enough to satisfy her. She was always looking for a better way to turn a dishonest dollar and get her hands on all the gold in a man's pocket. Then it dawned on her: If it was good enough for a guy named Cain in the good book, it should be good enough for her. Murder, anyone?

Steffleback was one of the more nefarious serial killers in nineteenth-century western history. Unfortunately, little is known about her. Many accounts offer more shadows than light, and information about her is hard to verify.

The southeastern corner of Kansas was hilly and rocky. As farmers would discover, the soil in the region was not as suitable for crops as in other parts of the state; sodbusters made a precarious living. But the area had long been known for its high concentration of lead. Early travelers would spot chunks lying on the ground. They would melt the ore over the campfire and mold the useful substance into rifle and pistol balls. By the mid-1870s, an enterprising farmer who owned some very lead-rich land convinced a local mining company to try to extract the material. Before long, the boomtown of Galena sprang up.

Soon more than 300 mines were established near Galena. By the early 1880s, there were more than 30,000 miners eager to make their fortunes. Galena boasted two banks, thirty-six grocery stores, and forty-eight other establishments. (Today, by comparison, Galena, Kansas, is a sleepy little town of 3,000.) There were enough gambling joints, whorehouses, and bars to keep an order of nuns praying for a decade. Ninety-proof lubrication, games of chance, and venal distractions were designed to separate men from their money as quickly as possible.

Fortunes were being made in Galena. At the peak of the mining boom in the 1890s, a quarter of all the lead and zinc in the world was mined in southeastern Kansas. The mines were almost as profitable as the combined profits of all the gold mines in the United States during that time.

In southeastern Kansas, it wasn't just the mining companies that got rich. While cooling off on a hot afternoon at a local swimming hole in Short Creek, a salty miner named Oll Sparks and a few friends found some chunks of curious-looking lead. He and his friends bummed tools from some fellow miners and started to dig. They sank a shaft twenty feet deep and found a rich vein. They called their new mine the Red Onion. The miners sold the claim for $20,000, and the rest is mining history. Within a short time, as many as 10,000 miners were seeking their destiny in the Short Creek area. Sparks went on to discover and develop many other mines, eventually selling them all for more than $220,000.

The flip side of such affluence was that it attracted the less savory elements: outlaws and bandits who loved to rob with a Colt or a Winchester. Other types of criminals made profits by hook and by crook. As the Galena *Sentinel* reported in a turn-of-the-century article:

> *The boys were high rollers in those days. Red Hot Street was the main thoroughfare and the scene of bloody action.*

Along this street were clustered haunts of dissipation and prostitution. Most frequented places were the Round Top, the Hickory Tree, the Log Cabin, and Dick Swapp's Place. In saloons the lewd and the reckless were congregated at all hours, intoxicated by wine, lulled . . . by siren's charms to commit deeds undreamed of under other circumstances.

Medical personnel took to sleeping during the day, and so did the undertakers. The town was so wild and business was so brisk, it was next to impossible to get any sleep at night.

Ma Steffleback's brothel, for one, was always busy. Steffleback was a confirmed miser and penny pincher. She didn't live any higher than she needed to in order to keep up appearances. She also liked to have control, so she wasn't about to marry the man she was living with, Charles Wilson.

According to local folklore, one night Steffleback saw a well-heeled miner pull gold out of his poke to pay for some pleasures, and a diabolical plan took hold. She would have one of her girls, a tart she trusted, get the man talking. If it looked like he wouldn't be missed, was a newcomer, or was a transient—and especially if he was carrying serious money—they'd get him sloppily drunk (or drugged if that was quicker) and lure him out of sight, where they could have some privacy.

When the coast was clear, Wilson or one of her sons would bash the man in the head with an ax, and Steffleback would rob him of all he was worth. She would go through the dead man's pockets herself. Then her male accomplice would stuff the body in a large canvas bag. They'd throw their victim on a horse or in a wagon and take him to one of the many abandoned mine shafts in the area and dump the corpse. No one would ever know.

For a while, Steffleback's plan worked quite well. Some say the madam murdered, robbed, and disposed of as many as fifty victims over a period of several years.

But eventually the scheme backfired. Steffleback got into a tiff with one of her working girls, a prostitute named Cora, and threw the woman out of the house. The problem was, Cora knew quite a bit about

Steffleback's extracurricular activities. Some believe she may have tried to blackmail Steffleback; others say she simply went straight to the sheriff. At any rate, Cora sang, and the law listened.

The authorities were particularly interested in Cora's story. Too many miners had been reported missing in the town. According to local accounts, Cora knew a few names and said that the last time she had seen so-and-so alive was in Ma Steffleback's "house of ill repute." The police followed up. And before long, Steffleback found herself in jail with Wilson and her sons.

Police searched for Steffleback's ill-gotten loot, but never found it. They searched empty mine shafts for discarded bodies, even draining some of the mines. Then they got lucky; searchers found the body of a miner named Frank Galbreath. Along with Cora's testimony, the physical evidence was enough to put Ma out of business for good.

In 1897, Steffleback, Charles Wilson, and her boys were convicted of Galbreath's murder. Steffleback was sentenced to the State Women's Prison at Lansing, Kansas. She spent twelve years behind bars until she died in 1909, proclaiming her innocence until the end. She never told anyone where she had hidden her blood money. Her brothel was carefully deconstructed to see if the loot or additional incriminating evidence could be found, but Ma Steffleback had been too clever. Because she was careful about burying her victims in different mine shafts, only two bodies were ever found.

Someday, perhaps, someone will find Steffleback's hidden gold. Her murders made history—as did her money. She didn't live high nor did she trust banks. Like the miser she was, she hoarded her money and kept it carefully hidden. Treasure seekers still look for her bloody loot, and her unrepentant ghost is said to haunt her fortune. ⟶

WESTERN LEGENDS

WOMEN
LARGER
THAN LIFE

CALAMITY JANE IS ONE OF THE MOST RECOGNIZABLE characters in American history. She was the nineteenth-century hero of dime novels and the darling of pulp fiction. To read about her exploits, one would assume she was Robin Hood, Jesse James, Mother Teresa, Indira Gandhi, and Wonder Woman rolled into one rope-throwing, Colt-carrying, horse-riding package. Her legendary exploits never seemed to end. But the truth was, there was absolutely no correlation between the Calamity Jane of song and story and the Martha Jane Canary who was an alcoholic, a prostitute, and a thief. She was no superhero; Canary lived a lonely, desperate life and often went to bed hungry.

Sally Skull, from southern Texas, was a crusty horsewoman who could crack her whip and take off your ear. She could also plug a running coyote with a Colt cap-and-ball revolver faster than you can wink. She was a better judge of horses than she was of men, however, and she had a string of husbands in a time when divorced women were considered social outcasts. Skull ran a ranch, raised cattle, sold horses, and traded cotton for guns in support of the Confederacy during the Civil War. Along the way, a few of her husbands seemed to "conveniently" disappear, and folks said she'd "done 'em in." So did she blast a few men? With Skull, anything seemed possible.

Elizabeth Bassett received little fanfare during her lifetime, but had she lived longer she might have become an American hero. As it was, she was a maverick homesteader who was denounced as a rustler at a time when large-scale Colorado and Wyoming ranch operations tried to take over her beloved rangeland. A pioneer in every sense of the word, Bassett came west across the Overland Trail, built a ranch, and battled to keep it. Her daughter Ann, known as the "Queen of the Rustlers," is likely more famous than her mother because of the legal wars she fought with one of the biggest ranchers in the region. Both Ann Bassett and her sister Josie also found fame as occasional cattle rustlers. Although lacking Elizabeth's moral fiber, her daughters kept her wild spirit alive. ⊷

CHAPTER THREE

CALAMITY JANE
The Facts *about the* Legend

E ven today, her name is synonymous with the American West. She was caught up in the vortex of fame, not really understanding what was happening. In the second half of the nineteenth century, Calamity Jane was one of the biggest celebrities in the United States. The Calamity Jane of pulp fiction and dime novels achieved icon status among the likes of Davy Crockett, Daniel Boone, George Custer, Wild Bill Hickok, and Buffalo Bill. She was characterized as brave and fearless, a unique brand of American hero.

The real-life Martha Jane Canary was nothing like her fictionalized counterpart. She was simply a down-on-her luck young woman, a drunken prostitute who happened to catch the eye of an enterprising journalist in 1875. Martha Jane became Calamity Jane, star of the media in the East. Ironically, her media persona created fortunes for her publishers, while the real Martha Jane Canary lived in abject poverty, frequently resorting to prostitution and petty theft to survive.

The oldest of six children, Martha Jane Canary was born May 1, 1852, in Princeton, Missouri. The young Martha Jane loved the outdoors.

She enjoyed fishing, riding, and hunting—and was no stranger to fire-arms. She behaved more like a farm boy than a young lady. She wasn't one for dresses and dolls and parlor-room chitchat, nor did she spend any time in school. Even at a young age, young Martha Jane could swear like a salty old muleskinner.

Just after the Civil War, her father got "Western Fever," so he packed up his family and headed for Montana. Martha Jane helped drive the wagon and shot game for the pot because her father was often drunk. She also learned how to use a "black snake," a bullwhip, as she urged the weary team along the trail. To make money along the way, her mother took in washing, and her father did odd jobs when they stopped to rest the team. In 1866 Martha Jane's mother died of pneumonia near Blackfoot, Montana. Her father decided to take his family to Salt Lake City in Utah Territory. In 1867 her father died there, leaving his young family destitute.

Young Martha Jane did her best to hold her family together, taking any job she could find. In 1868, she moved her family to Fort Bridger, Wyoming, in search of better employment. Not able to support her brothers and sisters, she found homes that would adopt the young orphans. It's unclear what she did for the next few years. In her autobi-ography, *The Life and Adventures of Calamity Jane*, she claims she rode south to Arizona with Lt. Col. George Armstrong Custer in 1870. This is a fabrication; Custer never went to Arizona.

In 1875 she tried to accompany the Dodge Expedition, which was headed to the Black Hills to look for gold. She attempted to find employment as a muleskinner for the group. However, her gender soon came to the attention of the authorities and she was sent home. In the spring of 1876 she accompanied Major General George Crook's expedi-tion in Montana—probably as a camp follower or a muleskinner, not as a scout as she later claimed. After leaving Montana a few months later, she found herself in Cheyenne, Wyoming, where she worked on a hog ranch, the lowest of whorehouses, and spent time in jail for stealing clothes.

In the summer of 1876, a group of men, including Wild Bill Hickok, were planning a trip to a brand-new boomtown in Dakota Territory called

Deadwood. Apparently, the frontiersmen needed companionship for the lonely nights spent on the trail. They also brought a few barrels of good whiskey. Being trail wise, and desperately in need of money, Calamity Jane agreed to go along as one of the prostitutes. The whiskey was a bonus.

When the group rode into Deadwood, the town cheered them. Lieutenant Colonel Custer had just been wiped out at the Battle of the Little Bighorn, and the town was anxious to have every extra gun. Bragging to a journalist after drinking too much, Calamity Jane extolled her fabricated adventures with the Custer, Dodge, and Crook expeditions, as well as the trip from Wyoming to Deadwood. Never letting the facts get in the way of a good story, her adventures were written as newspaper articles, short stories, and novels.

In print, Calamity Jane was a character of epic proportion. She was portrayed as a misunderstood heroine—a gunwoman in men's clothes who could ride, curse, drink, and use a bullwhip. Reporters had her saving wagon trains from marauding Plains Indians and bringing food to snowed-in ranchers in the dead of winter. She liked her notoriety, but after an interview and a few rounds of drinks—typically paid for by the writers and journalists—she'd go home to a sleazy crib (a low-end brothel), a barn, an abandoned cabin, or a rented room. When she did manage to make good money, she drank it up or gave it away.

Calamity Jane had many demons, the largest of which was the bottle. From an early age she showed all the signs of alcoholism, including severe binge drinking. Her lack of education didn't help: she could barely read or write, making it easy for people to take advantage of her. Her list of offenses included drunken and disorderly conduct, prostitution, shoplifting, running up store credit with no intention of paying, and running naked through the streets when drunk. She was not a very good shoplifter, considering how often she got caught. She spent a few nights in jail every now and then, mostly because she could not make bail.

When sober, she was gracious, even capable of great acts of service. She would help a fellow who was down and out, giving him her last dollar. In Deadwood in 1878, she helped nurse sick men from a smallpox epidemic—at great risk to herself. At one point Calamity Jane left the

Decked out in buckskins and armed to the teeth, Calamity Jane (Martha Jane Canary) poses for the camera. She tried to play the part of a frontier heroine, but her life was more tragedy than epic western drama.

town to help eight men who were so ill they couldn't leave their cabins. Three of the men died, whom she buried, but the other five lived.

She was sometimes photographed in buckskins or canvas pants, which is largely how she's remembered today. But the majority of photos from that time show her wearing a dress, following the standard practice of her day.

Beyond the bravado and hype, all she really wanted was a simple domestic life and to be a wife and a mother. She dreamed of a home in the country, with animals, children, and a loving husband.

One thing many don't know about this fascinating woman is that she was an excellent dancer. She occasionally worked as a dancehall girl, charging by the dance. A good dancer made far more than most prostitutes. She enjoyed trying to make a living as a dancer; however, before long she would get sloppy drunk and was fired. Most dancers were not allowed to drink, which was a problem for her. Around 1895, toward the end of her life, she was invited back to "Old Deadwood Days" in Deadwood, South Dakota. The men and boys lined up to dance with her, an American legend, for two bits a whirl. She could dance your legs off.

Had Calamity been able to handle her press like Buffalo Bill Cody, Custer, Annie Oakley, and, to some extent, Wild Bill Hickok, she could have had a lucrative career as a western personality. She had more publicity breaks than one could imagine, but she was never comfortable enough or clever enough to parlay it to her advantage.

As she struggled to put a roof over her head and food in her belly, writers built a legend and made her famous. She showed up in Magurie's 1877 *The Black Hills: An American Wonderland*, a travel book. The next year she was featured in *Drama of Life in the Black Hills*. She was further featured in the *Deadwood Dick* adventure series by Edward Wheeler. Nearly a decade later, in 1887, *Calamity Jane, A Story of the Black Hills*, by Mrs. William Spencer, was a best seller.

With all the attention surrounding her exploits, Calamity Jane was just the kind of attraction Buffalo Bill needed to draw in crowds to his wild west shows, and she was soon hired. However, like all the other good gigs she landed as a result of her pulp fame, the folks around her discovered that the woman had a hard time living up to her myth or even staying sober. Buffalo Bill didn't care about her drinking—he was a heavy drinker himself—but Bill's cardinal rule was that alcohol should never get in the way of show biz. Jane couldn't hold her Red Eye and was quickly a source of embarrassment to the show. Buffalo Bill hated to fire her, but he had to let her go. He ran a family show; Calamity Jane had proven to be a liability.

Calamity Jane joined other wild west shows, with predictable results. The woman who was billed as the "Heroine of a Thousand Thrilling Adventures" or "Terror of Evil Doers in the Black Hills" was a lush and bad for business. At the Pan American Expo in 1901, the worse for drink, she tried to have a knockdown with the city's finest officers. She lost.

She wrote her life story circa 1900, titled *The Life and Adventures of Calamity Jane*. Though popular, the book wasn't much of a moneymaker. She tried selling signed copies, but as soon as she made a little money, she'd end up in a bar.

She was good about perpetuating and validating the tall stories that had been written about her—rarely denying any adventure that appeared in print. One of her biggest fibs was her association with Wild Bill Hickok, whom she claimed was the love of her life. There are absolutely no facts to back up her claim, but the Calamity Jane fabric of multihued hyperbole is carelessly, although colorfully woven. Her supposed relationship with the legendary gunman was a big hit with eastern readers and is still a major strand in both Wild Bill and Calamity Jane legends.

The Calamity Jane of legend went to her grave carrying a torch for the long-haired pistol fighter. She often bragged how she'd like to put a bullet in Jack McCall, the coward who killed Wild Bill in 1876. She told how she had McCall trapped in a butcher shop and would have clawed his eyes out if the dang townsfolk hadn't drug her off him. The truth: Martha Jane did live in Deadwood, and she probably did say howdy now and again to the famous gunman. We do know she was one of the camp followers that came into town with Hickok and the soldiers. Beyond that is pure story time. Frankly, Jane was not the kind of girl the womanizing Wild Bill would have looked twice at unless he was falling down drunk— and probably not even then. But because Wild Bill was safely planted on boot hill, he was not able to set the record straight.

Despite what pulp fiction and dime novelists wrote, Calamity Jane and legendary scout, lawman, gunfighter, and gambler Wild Bill Hickok were never romantically involved. KANSAS STATE HISTORICAL SOCIETY, TOPEKA.

Calamity Jane stands at the grave of Wild Bill Hickok in Deadwood, South Dakota. She claimed to have attempted to avenge Hickok's murder in 1876: "I at once started to look for the assassian [sic] and found him at Shurdy's butcher shop and grabbed a meat cleaver and made him throw up his hands; through the excitement on hearing of Bill's death, having left my weapons on the post of my bed . . . he got away."
LIBRARY OF CONGRESS, PRINTS AND PHOTOGRAPHS DIVISION, LC-USZ62-47389.

Calamity Jane in Lewistown, Montana, in 1889. 941-414, MRS. E. G. WORDEN.
MONTANA HISTORICAL SOCIETY, HELENA.

Calamity Jane continued to struggle for stability and security for the rest of her life. Toward the end, an interviewer caught up with her. In a rare moment of sobriety, she reflected on her life. Normally she liked to spin outlandish tales. But on this day, she offered a gloomy introspection, "I ain't anybody, no how." In 1903, at age 51, she lost her long battle with alcohol, but her legend lives on. May she finally rest in peace. ⊷

Calamity Jane died in 1903 and is buried in Deadwood, South Dakota. Her grave-stone reads "Martha Jane Burke" because in her autobiography she claims to have married a man named Clinton Burke, although there is no record of this union. MICHAEL RUTTER.

CHAPTER FOUR

SALLY SKULL

Horse Trader, Gun Runner, AND Five-Time Wife

Everything is bigger in Texas—legends included. According to folklore, Sally Skull always packed a Bowie knife and a six-gun. It was said she could shoot the sweat off a fly at fifty feet. With a bullwhip, the old boys from border country claimed, she could pluck off the head of a flower—or snap off a man's earlobe.

Rumor has it she buried a few troublesome husbands who had the bad sense to get in her way. A Texas Ranger named Rip Taylor claimed he saw her shoot a man at a local fair. "A prudent man," he said, "did not willingly provoke her." Another observer, J. Frank Dobie, put it this way: "Sally Skull belonged to the days of the Texas Republic and afterwards. She was notorious for her husbands, her horse trading, freighting, and roughness." On one thing all agree: she was one tough customer.

She was born Sara Jane Newman in 1817, in Illinois Territory east of St. Louis. Her family called her Sally, and she was the youngest of ten children. In 1823 the Newman family, hoping to better their situation, loaded their possessions onto a wagon and moved to Fayette County, Texas. Like so many struggling ranch wives, Sally's mother, Rachel, was left alone while her husband fought Indians, drove cattle, and worked on the range. Sally's father, Joseph, was apparently so busy he'd neglected to hang the front door properly on their cabin. One evening, during an Indian raid on the Newman homestead, a brave managed to stick his foot through a gap in the door and tried to make his way inside. Rachel picked up an ax and summarily chopped off all his toes.

There are few reliable accounts from that time, but according to local lore, Sally shot her first man when she was still a young girl. Apparently, she and her mother were alone on the ranch when one of them spotted some Indians sneaking up. Their cabin was on one of the most remote ranches in Austin's struggling settlement. Sally picked up a rifle, used some "Kentucky windage," and plugged the stealthy warrior with a lead ball.

By the time Sally was twelve, she was said to ride and shoot skillfully and bring in venison and wild hog for the family table. She also had an affinity for livestock—especially horses, the great love of her life—and she learned the art of horse trading at a young age.

With her father gone so often, she helped in the fields and with the livestock. When her father died in 1831, fourteen-year-old Sally was running the family ranch handily. She divided up the livestock with her brother, who had little interest in ranching, and registered her father's brand in her own name. She was more than capable of running stock.

In 1833, at age sixteen, Sally fell in love and married a dashing Texas Ranger named Jess Robinson. They settled in nearby Gonzales, Texas. As a Texas Ranger, Robinson was rarely home. Sally managed the cattle and horse herds nicely without him.

Sally and her husband, both independent sorts, had a tempestuous relationship at best. They managed to quit fighting long enough to produce two children: Nancy and Alfred. But in 1843, after almost ten years of unhappiness, they filed for divorce. Scandalous as divorce was in those days, Sally soon made an even bolder move; on March 17, 1843, just eleven days after the divorce went through, she married a gunsmith named George Scull (she would keep this name for the rest of her life but spelled it Skull, instead). If she thought she was done with Jess Robinson, though, she was mistaken. For the next few years, the custody battle over Nancy and Alfred was intense. Sally finally prevailed, but it took all her savings.

As gruff as Sally Skull was, she loved her children and did her best to be a good mother. Because she was illiterate, and a bit ashamed of it, she saw to it that her son and daughter had excellent educations in New Orleans. She chose New Orleans partly for its schools, and partly because the distance would further insulate them from their father.

Her marriage to George Scull, though, was little more than another shouting match. Sally was stubborn and opinionated; she had helped run her father's ranch from an early age and didn't need a man telling her what to do. The couple made an effort to live together, but the marriage was a failure—and would soon end in mystery. In 1849, Sally started telling people that George had died. It was never known whether he ran off, was kicked out, faked his own death, or had actually died. The rumor was that the fiery woman shot Scull in a fit of anger, but charges were never filed.

By 1852 Sally Skull had moved to a ranch closer to the border, near Banquete, Texas. Her business was thriving. She had become a successful horse trader, traveling into Mexico and back to do business. She spoke fluent Spanish and was able to curse with proficiency in both her first and second languages.

In October of 1852, she married a third time, to a man named John Doyle. It wasn't a good match. Before long, Doyle simply disappeared. Once again, it was suggested she was responsible. Some say she shot him, or perhaps tried to drown him in a barrel full of whiskey (Doyle liked to drink). Others say Doyle lost his life taking horses across a fast-moving river; he was unseated and swept away by the current. Skull is reported to have said, "I don't give a damn about the body . . . sure'd like to have the gold in his money belt."

Apparently, Isaiah Wadkins hadn't heard about Skull's record with husbands, or didn't care. Wadkins married her on December 26, 1855, and things quickly went sour. Skull's fourth husband beat her up and openly played house with a prostitute named Juanita. Wadkins was so blatant about his affair that he was indicted for adultery by a grand jury. She again divorced.

Not one to let a few lousy marriages get her down, Skull would shortly try again. In December of 1860, a year before the start of the

Civil War, she married husband number five. She was in her forties and he in his twenties. His name was Christopher Horsdorff, but he went by the name "Horse Trough."

The marriage, and life in general, was changed drastically by war. Some seventy-five percent of Texans sided with the South and were in favor of secession. Texans had a tradition of fighting. In recent years they had fought the bloody war with Mexico; they were constantly skirmishing with the Comanche and other warring Indian tribes. Texans had defeated Santa Anna, established a republic, and joined the Union—one they felt they had a right to leave. They weren't about to be told what to do by eastern politicians and bureaucrats.

Volunteers for the Confederacy streamed out of backwater bayous, frontier cattle ranches, and coastal farms. The Union had the Southern harbors bottled up so that raw goods could not move in or out. But Union ships could not shut down trade with Mexico. Austin, San Antonio, and Houston became thriving trade centers. Traders shipped raw goods by rail or loaded them onto wagons and transported them south. Merchants allegedly shipped so many bales of cotton that the chaparral along the road north of Brownsville appeared to be blanketed with snow. The Cotton Road, which extended from just east of Houston south through Banquete and into Mexico, was a main trade artery for the Confederacy.

This was Skull's country, and she knew it well. Her ranch at Banquete was conveniently located near the Cotton Road. She was a Texan first, but she was also a loyal Confederate. She was familiar with Mexico and its merchants, thanks to her years in horse trading. Like many Texas women, she also took on new responsibilities for the cause—and started trading goods and running guns for the South. She didn't mind leaving her husband at home when duty called. By the time war broke out, she'd realized her new spouse wasn't much better than her old ones. Before long, he would disappear, too.

But if romance was a bust, business was good. Demand for cotton was high. It was illegal for businesses in the Union to purchase raw materials from Confederate state; however because of the Cotton Road, large amounts of Texas cotton made their way to Union mills under a Mexican flag. The black market thrived. And money from cotton sales brought

During the Civil War, Sally Skull drove cotton wagons, similar to this one, from Texas to Mexico on the infamous Cotton Road. The Confederates traded cotton with Mexico to avoid Union blockades. After selling a shipment of cotton to Mexican merchants, Confederate cotton wagon masters purchased supplies and brought them back to Texas for distribution. TEXAS STATE LIBRARY AND ARCHIVES COMMISSION.

the South what it desperately needed: military hardware and medicine. (The Union had halted all medical supplies, specifically anesthetics, from reaching the enemy.) Skull would leave Texas with ten bales of cotton on each of her sturdy wagons, pulled by teams of ten to twelve oxen or six to eight mules. Her Mexican cowboys would serve as her muleskinners, drivers of the mule team.

The Cotton Road was not without peril, however, especially on the return trip. After the goods were sold in Mexico, the wagons would be loaded with guns or other useful items. The medium of exchange was always gold. Willing to steal the gold and guns were marauding bands of Indians, bandits, Union troops, and Jayhawkers (antislavery guerrillas in Kansas and Missouri), among others.

It was a dangerous time, and one was always at risk. No wonder Skull and other skinners traveled heavily armed. John Warren Hunter, who knew Skull, comments on this in his book *Heel-Fly Time in Texas,* published in 1931. Hunter writes that "[She wore] a black dress and a sunbonnet, sitting erect as a cavalry officer, with a six-shooter hanging at her belt." No doubt she had a rifle and a scattergun nearby, too.

In the end, Skull was a study in contrasts. She sported a flea-bitten sunbonnet and made her living on the range, but she made sure her children got fine educations. She failed in marriage, but she was a proud mother; she never lost contact with her children and helped them as much as she could. Her daughter Nancy lived in Blanconia, Texas, near the Cotton Road, so Skull visited often. She also tried to help her son Alfred, who had a ranch about twenty-five miles away and fought with the Confederate cavalry.

We also know that she served the Southern cause valiantly until the war's end. What happened to Skull in the post-war years has baffled historians for decades because few official records about Skull can be found. In 1868, her son Alfred, along with Nancy's two sons, recorded her brand in Nueces County, Texas, which suggests that Skull had died: the children probably wouldn't have assumed her brand if she were alive. Some say Skull was later seen in western Texas, shooting holes in coins pitched into the air, but this can't be proven.

The most plausible story, historians say, is that Skull met her fate at the hands of her fifth husband, Christopher Horsdorff, who may have killed her for her money. It appears she'd set aside a good sum from her gun-running days. According to folklore, on a business trip to Mexico, "Horse Trough" put a bullet in her head and buried her in a shallow grave. He took her gold and goods, and disappeared. As J. Frank Dobie suggests in *A School Teacher in Alpine*, "Sally belongs to the days of the Texas Republic . . . her death remains as much a mystery as most of her life." ⇥

CHAPTER FIVE

ELIZABETH, JOSIE, AND ANN BASSETT

The Wild Women ▧ Brown's Park

The Bassett women had a profound, enduring love for the land they settled. The West never raised a spicier, more spirited trio of ranch women: Elizabeth, the strong, visionary matriarch of the clan, and her two mercurial daughters, Josie and Ann. They were women who would not be tamed. Detractors have called them rustlers, horse thieves, and prostitutes. But they were, first and last, women of terra firma, fearless when protecting what was theirs.

Elizabeth Bassett

In 1877 Herb and Elizabeth Bassett headed west for California on the Overland Trail with their two small children. However, in Green River, Wyoming, they decided to detour south and visit Herb's brother, who had a trapper's cabin in a mountain valley on the Green River. The country seemed to stretch on forever, a land for the taking if you were bold enough to try. Herb wanted to continue on to California, but

Elizabeth had found her Eden and refused to take their wagon another foot. With her sweat and blood, she began constructing a home in which to raise their children.

Not much of a rancher, Herb was happy to watch the kids. He tended the garden and ran the household while Elizabeth built the ranch. When Ann was born, the Bassetts hired an Indian woman to wet-nurse the infant.

The family fought predators and the elements. Elizabeth shot wild game for the pot while they built cattle and horses herds. The Ute Indians taught them how to make jerky, what plants to harvest, and how to catch fish. The first few years were very hard, but each year their homestead improved.

Elizabeth and her husband were among the first homesteaders to settle a lonely piece of the Colorado Plateau known to trappers and itinerants as Brown's Hole. The valley was five miles wide and thirty miles long. It was perfect cattle country, with sweet grass, good water, and mountains to shelter the range during the coldest winter months. Elizabeth Bassett insisted that it should be called Brown's Park. Her valley was too lovely "to be referred to as a hole"—even if "hole" in western parlance meant "valley." She thought her ranch, located near the borders of Utah, Colorado, and Wyoming, was the most perfect place on earth.

Elizabeth's relationship with her husband was certainly unconventional for their day. She had read a great deal on feminism and possessed a library of books on the subject. She was not concerned with traditional gender roles, and she continued to run the ranch while her husband read books and schooled their children.

As much as Elizabeth loved ranch life, Herb missed the people and culture of larger towns. He was a gifted musician, and sometimes Elizabeth would return from the range to the sounds of violin or organ music. In spite of their differences, they loved each other and were content. If Elizabeth was happy, Herb was happy.

Elizabeth was the kind of woman who would stand up and fight for what she believed. Although bold and in control, she was also kind and commanded loyalty from those around her. Her children worshiped her.

She was well-liked by her neighbors and loved by the ranch hands, whom she treated like family.

In 1879, the Bassetts' blissful life was shaken up. A clash had been brewing between Ute Indians and officials from the White River Agency, about sixty-five miles from Brown's Park. The tribe's annuities had not arrived, and supplies were desperately needed if the Utes were going to make it through the winter. There was also a bitter ongoing argument about how the U.S. government was hacking away at Indian land and giving it to settlers. On September 29, 1879, members of the tribe attacked the White River Agency; Indian agent Nathan Meeker was found near his cabin with a chain about his neck and his head bashed in. At least eight other settlers were also killed.

News of the massacre quickly spread throughout the region, including Brown's Park. Many residents packed up and went to Green River or Rock Springs, Wyoming, to ride out the hostilities. Elizabeth had different ideas. Not wanting to lose what she had worked so hard for, she intended to stay on the land and let Herb take the kids to town. This was perhaps the first time in their married life that Herb put his foot down. He insisted that she leave, and Elizabeth reluctantly agreed, looking back on her little ranch, wondering tearfully if the buildings would be burned to the ground by the time she returned.

The Bassetts stayed in Rock Springs for more than a year while the U.S. Army sorted out the dispute with the Ute tribe. Cooped up in a small makeshift apartment, Elizabeth was more than ready to get back to her ranch. She had big plans, which included constructing barns, bunkhouses, corrals, fences, and, of course, building up the cattle and horse herds.

When Elizabeth returned home, she found her land had been spared and the cabin and buildings were still intact. She jumped right back into her arduous routine, tirelessly working to grow the ranch. She placed particular focus on her passion: raising a line of excellent thoroughbred horses. Bassett horses were some of the best animals in the region. Always cash poor, she and Herb poured every cent back into the ranch. Contentedly, she watched her children grow and her land become more productive, while Herb grew an excellent garden and planted an orchard.

In the 1880s pressures from outside the valley were starting to build. Using the 1879 "Meeker Massacre" as an excuse, land speculators and ranchers insisted that the government move the "hostile" Indians elsewhere and open up vast tracts of fertile land for settlement. Large cattle monopolies, often with European backing, were among the first to gobble up the best sections of land, creating ranching fiefdoms that rivaled medieval baronies. Such expansion would bring an inevitable conflict with the smaller ranchers and homesteaders in Brown's Park, who, up until this time, had been left to their own resources. Elizabeth's quiet valley was about to become a political, if not a literal, battlefield, as the big cattle interests banded together to run out the Brown's Park inhabitants.

The big cattle companies, with the support of the powerful Wyoming Stock Growers Association (WSGA), pulled political strings and used strong-arm tactics to get their way. In addition to their influence in state government and the law enforcement community, the big ranchers essentially controlled the newspapers—and, thus, public opinion.

The WSGA criminalized its prey before striking, so that its actions looked justified. They accused Brown's Park residents—and, earlier, residents of nearby Johnson County—of being cattle rustlers and would thereby appear justified when they asked to have them removed from the valley. The large ranchers knew it was important, morally and legally, to appear to be in the right. The homesteaders, meanwhile, ended up looking like outlaws.

One of the biggest ranches in the Brown's Park area was the Middlesex Land and Cattle Company, known as the Flying VD. It was owned by Boston investors and was located twenty-five miles away from the Bassett spread. Another threat was a cattleman from Laramie. The ambitious Ora Haley of the Two Bar Ranch was buying up ranches and former Indian land to build one of the largest empires in the West.

The presence of these large ranches was altering the culture of the cattle range. Historically, cattle roundups had been a community affair: All the cattle in a region were gathered, and each rancher's stock was sorted according to brand. But now the big ranches were sweeping up all the cattle in their paths, no matter what the brand, and mingling the stock with their own.

Elizabeth Bassett knew this practice was intended to intimidate the homesteaders and drive them out of business. But Brown's Park residents did not scare easily, and Bassett led the charge. She knew that if they went on the offensive, there was chance of bloodshed. Association ranches had hired a lot of hands, and some were gunmen. She decided to take another approach: band together as a unit to prevent the large ranches from grazing their land; some of the Brown's Park ranchers also decided to rustle from the big herds to get even.

Some of the most wanted outlaws in the West already used Brown's Park as a place to hold over between jobs. The small ranchers, who were treated like outlaws anyway, developed a symbiotic relationship with men on the run who sought refuge in the valley. Outlaw rustlers would steal beef from the association ranchers and sell it to their ready-made market. Local ranchers bought the cattle at low prices to increase their herds. Outlaws were given refuge as long as they didn't bother any Brown's Park herds or cause trouble. Many of the outlaws were excellent hands who enjoyed living with a ranch family for room and board while they "cooled off."

Desperados, including some who would later be called the Wild Bunch, frequented the Bassett ranch. Butch Cassidy himself was a valued Bassett ranch hand and close friend of the family, as was the Sundance Kid. Other well-known men on the dodge, including Elza Lay and Matt Warner, visited Brown's Park and the Bassett home. The men took jobs as cowboys for room and board and, if they were lucky, a small wage. They were considered part of the family.

Elizabeth Bassett hired excellent ranch hands. She could not pay a lot, but her food was good, and her horses were excellent. Some of her hands, she knew, were expert gunmen. Butch Cassidy was a Mormon who had drifted from his God-fearing upbringing. By the mid-1880s, he was on the wrong side of the law. Nevertheless, he was a top stockman and a first-rate cowboy, loyal to any outfit he rode for. Although he was considered a rustler, he was never dishonest with his employers. He was a Bassett family favorite. Cassidy was quite intelligent and well read and enjoyed losing himself in the Bassett library. He looked up to Elizabeth as an older sister. He played with the Bassett children and was a great help around the ranch.

Butch Cassidy (Robert LeRoy Parker) worked as a ranch hand on the Bassett ranch. He was also the leader of the outlaw gang known as the Wild Bunch. This photo was taken while he was in prison for one of their many heists, as evidenced by his striped prison pants. WYOMING STATE ARCHIVES, DEPARTMENT OF STATE PARKS AND CULTURAL RESOURCES, 187.

After Butch Cassidy robbed the Telluride Bank in Colorado in 1889 and emerged with a big price on his head, he went on the lam. To hide, he kept a low profile at the Bassett ranch as a hired hand.

Matt Rash and Isom Dart were among some of Elizabeth Bassett's favorite ranch hands. A horse trainer, Dart was a freed slave who came up to Brown's Park with a Texas herd and stayed in the area. He was a gentle man who loved to play with the Bassett children and was one of Elizabeth's trusted friends. Dart was also a first-rate brand doctor. He had a gift for altering a brand on a rustled cow with a red-hot saddle ring. He had once been indicted in Sweetwater County, Wyoming, but was never brought to court.

Matt Rash was Dart's saddle partner and had also come up from Texas. He had worked for the Circle K until the ranch was put out of business by the expanding Flying VD. He never lost his hatred of the Flying VD. He liked to brag that many of the cows in his herd came from the Two Bar and Fly VD ranches. He also bragged that at his table, a guest would always be served beef—but never from his herd. He liked to sing, "We thank God for our bread and Ora Ben Haley for our beef."

Both Rash and Dart started out as Bassett hands while they built small spreads of their own nearby. Soon the three ranchers were running their herds together, each helping the others as needed, especially during branding and roundup time. The rancher-controlled press called Elizabeth Bassett, Isom Dart, and Matt Rash the Bassett Gang, one of the most effective group of rustlers in the Rocky Mountain region.

Although it's not known exactly how much cattle rustling went on under Elizabeth's direction, Dart and Rash had helped themselves to cattle from the larger ranches. Elizabeth wasn't above taking home a stray, especially if it didn't have a brand, and even more so if it might belong to the Two Bars, but she wasn't the stock thief she was made out to be.

In December of 1892, at the age of thirty-seven, Elizabeth Bassett died suddenly. Eldest daughter Josie believed she died of complications due to a pregnancy, and Ann thought her death was caused by a burst appendix. We'll never know for sure. Her death, however, was a shock to the family and their friends. Everyone looked to Elizabeth for strength, and her passing left a vacuum. To some extent her daughters never

Freed slave Isom Dart was a kindhearted horse trainer and one of Elizabeth Bassett's favorite ranch hands; he helped the local ranchers fight the Two Bar and Flying VD ranches. DENVER PUBLIC LIBRARY, WESTERN HISTORY COLLECTION, X-21560.

A group of Brown's Park cowboys, with Isom Dart at the center.
DENVER PUBLIC LIBRARY, WESTERN HISTORY COLLECTION, X-21559.

recovered. Elizabeth was surely the only one who could keep the girls in check.

After Bassett's death the cattle rustling escalated. The big ranchers and the WSGA had grown tired of losing cattle to the smaller ranchers of Brown's Park, especially to Dart and Rash, and they hired Tom Horn to take drastic measures. Horn was a famed tracker, man hunter, and professional killer who plied his trade with an Old Testament sense of justice. Horn pretended to be a cattleman/horse buyer named Hicks. He left notes on the doors of everyone who was suspected of rustling, including Dart's and Rash's cabins. The notes told the occupants to get out of the valley or they'd be killed.

Matt Rash was soon found dead lying in his bunk; Rash's horse had also been shot. It was rumored that Horn had even taken the time to put Rash in his bunk and take his boots off. Later that fall, Isom Dart met the same fate. Near each murdered man were empty .30-.30 shells, and a rock was placed under each man's head. All were Horn's calling cards; he was paid $500 for each rustler he killed. After these murders,

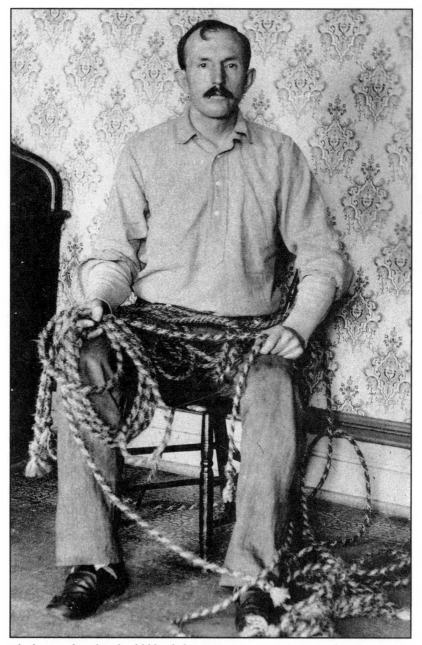

The big ranchers hired cold-blooded assassin Tom Horn to intimidate Brown's Park ranchers and put an end to the cattle rustling. DENVER PUBLIC LIBRARY, WESTERN HISTORY COLLECTION, F-7328.

rustling in Brown's Park dropped dramatically. The Bassett family was in shock over the killings, especially Ann, who some think might have been engaged to Rash.

Josie Bassett

From the time she was a little girl, Elizabeth Bassett's oldest daughter, Josie Bassett, loved ranch life. She loved working with stock and feeling the sun on her back and the wind in her hair. She started hunting as soon as she was big enough to hold a rifle. She was on a horse almost from the time she could walk, following her mother around the ranch. Josie loved her father, and they were close, but her mother had always been her role model. Josie had a fiery temper and was not above tantrums, but they blew over fast. At one point she went to a girls' school to finish her education.

In her later years she tells about meeting Butch Cassidy when she was fifteen years old:

> I thought he was the most dashing and handsome man I ever seen. I was such a young thing . . . and looked upon Butch as my knight in shining armor. He was more interested in his horse than he was in me, and I remember being very put off by that. I went home after being snubbed by him and stamped my foot in frustration.

She also suggests that Cassidy was a man who liked books and loved to read. Apparently, Cassidy slept in the barn when he was working for the Bassetts. Because of the fire danger, he was the only one who had the privilege of having a lantern so he could read after dark. When some men rode into the ranch looking for the "family outlaw," Josie told him to hide in the hay. He said he might get bored. Josie said she replied, "Well, all I can say is I didn't let him get bored."

What Elizabeth didn't know before she died was that eighteen-year-old Josie was pregnant by Joseph McKnight, the ranch foreman. The couple married on March 21, 1893, four months before the baby was born. The relationship proved to be an unhappy one, however.

Josie Bassett.

Josie would ultimately be married five times and have a string of lovers. She was known to have a wicked temper and never shy away from a fight. It was rumored that she took a shot at her first husband, McKnight; it was also said that she poisoned another husband, Nig Wells. Josie claimed both were lies. Wells had a serious drinking problem, so she had ordered a potion from Salt Lake City called the Keen Cure, which was supposed to keep a man on the wagon. She slipped her spouse some of the cure one night and he never woke up. Josie was never formally charged with her husband's murder, but there was suspicion surrounding his death.

After Wells' death, she married a fellow named Ben Morris. After clearing brush one day, they were a little tired and on edge. Morris complained that he had a few lumps in his gravy. Josie's temper flared and she gave him fifteen minutes to pack his belongings and get out. Knowing something of Josie's temper, Morris bragged, "I was packed and out of there in five minutes!"

Josie continued to live on her small ranch near Cub Creek, just over the mountains from Brown's Park. She supplemented her income by selling bootlegged whiskey and apricot brandy, although she drank very little herself. She poached mule deer, and she was never above taking a cow or two on the sly.

It wasn't until Josie was sixty-two years old that she finally got caught red-handed as she carved up someone else's beef in her barn. On the day of her 1911 trial, she pinned her hair up and wore her best dress, leaving her favorite attire—coveralls—hanging on a peg. "I'm a grandma—do I look like a cattle thief?" she said to the judge, her silver hair piled in a bun on her head and a kindly smile on her face. The charges were dropped, and Josie went home and continued to take cattle as she saw fit.

On a cold December morning in 1963, eighty-nine-year-old Josie stoked the fire in her cabin and grabbed a bucket to go to the spring for some water. On her way back, she fell and broke her hip. Crawling to her front door, she was so thirsty she drank water out of her dog's bowl. She was discovered by some friends who were scheduled to pick her up for a Christmas visit with her family. She was taken to the hospital in Vernal, Utah, but was later sent to a hospital in Salt Lake to have her broken bone pinned. She would never return to her beloved Cub Creek ranch, dying not long after her fall.

Over the course of her long life, she walked the Overland Trail behind a wagon, survived Indian attacks, homesteaded in the wilderness, knew some of the most famous outlaws of the Old West, and saw world wars and the advent of airplanes. The semi-arid landscape, grassy river valleys, grazing livestock, red rocks, snowcapped mountains, cool western breezes in the spring and autumn, and the heat in August were her truest loves, as they were her mother's.

Today, visitors can get a drink of water at her spring, look at her cabin, and walk about her spread. Her ranch is off a dusty road in Dinosaur National Park, near Vernal, Utah.

Ann Bassett

Ann Bassett was called the "Queen of the Rustlers," a title she enjoyed and tried to perpetuate. But she wasn't much of an outlaw. In fact, some would say she was just a temperamental brat who liked to play at being a rancher.

Ann loved to ride horses, but she didn't like dirt under her fingernails. Unlike her mother or sister, she was never one to get blisters on her hands and sweat on her face after an afternoon of digging postholes, mending fences, or branding calves. She left those jobs to someone else. She loved the land, but not like her mother or Josie did.

Both Ann and Josie were well educated and widely read. Both girls had gone to boarding school. But while Josie was a good student, Ann did not fare well and was considered a problem. She was impulsive and capricious—hard to control and, at times, hard to believe. After one of her trips out of town, she shocked the locals by dressing in the latest fashions and painting her cheeks red—something only bawdy women did. She also tried affecting a New England accent. A ranch girl from the toes of her cowboy boots to the top of her brunette head, she impressed the simplest ranch folk and amused the more cosmopolitan.

But as superficial as Ann sometimes seemed, she was also a maverick. She loved Brown's Park and never forgave the ranchers who fought her

Ann Bassett, known as the "Queen of the Rustlers."
DENVER PUBLIC LIBRARY, WESTERN HISTORY COLLECTION, X-153.

mother and tried to take their home. When Ann was twenty-five years old, she saw a chance to get back at the Two Bar Ranch for its collective sins. She flirted with the ranch manager, Hi Bernard, one of the most influential people at the Two Bar. She knew that ranch-owner Ora Haley would not be pleased if his manager consorted with "the enemy." Despite the talk, the two married in 1904. Bernard was promptly fired from the Two Bar Ranch.

The marriage was not a happy one. It seemed it was a six-year preview of hell before they finally divorced. Poor Bernard soon discovered that his new wife was prone to screaming tantrums, insisting that she always get her way.

To make matters worse, in 1911, the last year of their marriage, Ann was caught with Two Bar livestock—apparently the second phase of her Two Bar revenge program. She then used irrigation ditches to cut off critical water supplies to the Two Bar Ranch.

This was the last straw, and the Two Bar went into action, hoping to convict Ann so they could settle the water issue and run the Bassetts out of Brown's Park forever. The pushed for and got a quick trial date. The local folks, always in the mood for a good trial, rented an opera hall in Craig, Colorado, so there would be enough room to watch the proceedings. It was during her trial that a newspaper reporter dubbed her the "Queen of the Rustlers" and "Queen Ann." She was secretly pleased with both sobriquets, which followed her throughout her life.

The jury, which was composed of small homesteaders and ranchers, sided with what appeared to be a poor woman trying to save her land and water from the gluttonous cattlemen. Ann was acquitted.

After spending a lot of money and losing an embarrassing battle, the Two Bar desperately claimed to reporters that every one of the jury members had rustled beef and thus couldn't be impartial. The stubborn owner of the Two Bar, Ora Haley, refused to give up. So the Two Bar took the case to court again. This time, Ann's lawyer made a fool of Haley on the witness stand about how he'd cheated on his taxes. It didn't help, either, that the Two Bar foreman, another key witness, got himself fatally ventilated by a .45 slug during a shooting match with a lawman before he got a chance to testify.

Ann, meanwhile, became an even bigger local celebrity for standing up against the powerful rancher. When Ann was again acquitted, the headlines of the *Denver Post* read: "Business Closes, Bands Blare—Town of Craig Goes Wild With Joy." In Craig there were bonfires and an all-night dance to celebrate.

In her later years, Ann found true love. She married in 1923 and moved throughout the West with her husband, Frank Willis. Ann and Josie saw each other often. Ann, who had no children, was a devoted aunt to Josie's children. Ann died in 1956 at the age of seventy-eight.

Today, Ann is probably the best-known Bassett. But her mother and sister certainly deserve to share the billing. The Bassett women have become a part of our national outlaw history—celebrated for doing wrong. More than 100 years later, perhaps it's time to clear their names—and celebrate their lives. ↤

WOMEN, GALLOWS, AND LYNCH MOBS

DEATH BY HANGING
FOR THE
INNOCENT AND GUILTY

STRINGING UP A WOMAN, NO MATTER WHAT HER alleged offense, was a big deal in the Old West. Women were rarely, if ever, executed. Putting a noose on a female simply violated a westerner's sense of propriety.

A uniquely western notion of womanhood had developed on the frontier, shaping the way men thought about women and how they should be punished if they committed a crime. This ideology was part male chauvinism, part medieval chivalry—mingled with Victorian values and Christian dogma. In one sense, men believed that women—the "weaker sex"—shouldn't be punished for capital crimes because they weren't capable of that level of responsibility. Frontier men knew their female counterparts could be fiercely independent and tough, but hanging seemed too distinctly, well, unfeminine. Western discomfort with the notion might also have to do with the fact that women had been so scarce for so long in the Old West that wasting one on the hangman seemed a sin. Most western men thought it simply wasn't right to stretch a lady's neck no matter what she'd done.

More often than not, if a man and a woman committed a murder, the man could plan on a date with the gallows, but the woman would be found guilty of a lesser offense and most likely spared. If a woman was found guilty of murder, she'd probably do prison time.

Hanging a woman in the East, however, while not a common occurrence, did occur with more frequency than it did in the West. Many of the eastern states automatically included a hanging penalty if a criminal was convicted of a homicide—gender wasn't a criteria. A number of women paid the ultimate price.

One of the few women sentenced by a western court to hang was Elizabeth Potts, the first woman hanged in Nevada. Many Elko residents opposed the punishment, but they could not sway the courts to give her life imprisonment. A lynch mob was responsible for the death of Ellen Watson, the first woman hanged in Wyoming. The West tested its morality in both cases, and meted out justice— and injustice—that equaled what it gave to men. ⇥

CHAPTER SIX

ELIZABETH POTTS
Nevada's FIRST Woman
Executed ⚡ Hanging

It was Friday, March 15, 1890, when the jury solemnly returned to the Elko, Nevada, courtroom. It was not quite 8:00 P.M., and they had been conferring for less than four hours. The Honorable Judge Bigelow was presiding. He asked if the jury had reached a verdict, and indeed they had: The jurors found Josiah and Elizabeth Potts guilty of the murder of Miles Faucett. Five days later, Bigelow passed his sentence. Josiah and Elizabeth Potts, the husband and wife who stood before him, would be hanged by the neck until dead. "The mind naturally recoils with horror at the thought that anyone can become so lost to the common instincts of humanity," the judge pronounced, chiefly addressing Elizabeth. "To her, we look to everything that is gentle and kind . . . we can scarcely conceive her capable of committing the highest crime."

A special "double gallows" was built for the couple in Placerville, California, a town with a history so checkered it was once known as "Hangtown." The gallows was shipped by rail to Elko, where it was reconstructed near the courthouse, tested, and proclaimed ready.

On June 20, 1890, the condemned each took a long, stiff drink in

Elko law enforcement officials ready the gallows for the Pottses' executions in 1890.
NEVADA HISTORICAL SOCIETY, RENO.

their jail cells. Josiah was in his best suit, and Elizabeth wore a white dress with black bows. A preacher came to pray with them. Just after 10:30 A.M., they were escorted by Sheriff Barnard to the scaffold. Some fifty journalists and law enforcement officials were invited to witness the event; hanging a woman was considered too gruesome for the general public. Before them, Elizabeth once again proclaimed her innocence, but she refused to show emotion. On the scaffold the couple was reported to have kissed and shook hands. Their shoes were removed and their legs and hands bound. Hoods were placed over their heads. And at 10:44 A.M., both fell into eternity. Elizabeth was nearly decapitated by the drop. Josiah quivered a few times and was still. Both were officially

On June 20, 1890, Elizabeth Potts was the first woman in Nevada to die on the gallows.
NEVADA HISTORICAL SOCIETY, RENO.

pronounced dead and cut down a few minutes later. They were buried at about noon.

Elizabeth Potts thus became the first woman in Nevada to be executed by hanging. Outside state borders, the press signaled its support. "It is to the credit of Elko, Nevada, that it hangs a woman guilty of murder," stated an editorial in the *San Francisco Daily Report* a few weeks after the event. "It is a dreadful thing to hang a woman, but not so dreadful as for a woman to be a murderer."

But in Nevada, not all residents felt so sanguine. Hanging a woman was an anomaly in the West, and many locals recoiled at the execution. They felt that hanging a woman, no matter what her offense, was simply going too far. As the Elko newspaper, the *Weekly Independent*, put it in a June 13, 1890, editorial, hanging Potts "would not reflect any credit on Elko." Editorial writers at the paper felt that Josiah and Elizabeth Potts were guilty as charged but believed Josiah should hang because he was a man and more accountable; Elizabeth, the "weaker vessel," should spend her life in prison because she was a woman. Had the newspaper been able to see into the future, it might have posted this, too: The truth about the Pottses was stranger than fiction. And the facts uncovered after their deaths were strangest of all.

Elizabeth (her last name is unknown) was born in Manchester, England, on December 21, 1842. As a young woman, she met and fell in love with Josiah Potts. They married in 1863. Josiah was a small man who was said to have a gentle temper. The domineering Elizabeth was built like a bull rider, had piercing blue eyes, a smooth complexion, a stern look, and a mind of her own. In 1865 they came to the United States. The couple had five children, all but two of whom (for reasons unknown) were later adopted by other families. After some moving about, the family settled in a rented house in Carlin, Nevada, not far from Elko, where Josiah worked for the railroad.

Life wasn't always easy, economically or otherwise. At some point the couple had so many difficulties that Elizabeth left town and they separated. But she eventually returned and the two patched things up. Later, to make ends meet, they took on a boarder in the late spring and summer of 1887, an Englishman named Miles Faucett. Faucett not only paid for his room and board but also loaned them money. He eventually bought a ranch and moved out; he remained friendly with the couple and stayed with them when he was in town. At some point, however, there was a falling out over the money he had loaned them. The Pottses apparently had not made good on what they had borrowed.

On New Year's Eve 1888, Faucett stopped at the Pottses' home to try and collect; he brought along a friend, J. P. Linebarger, to lend support if things went sour. The Pottses invited Faucett in for a few drinks, acting

Josiah Potts was hanged with his wife, Elizabeth, in Elko, Nevada, for the murder and partial dismemberment of Miles Faucett. NEVADA HISTORICAL SOCIETY, RENO.

like they were old friends. Faucett, no longer feeling threatened, waved Linebarger on and went into the house alone.

Miles Faucett was never seen again. The Pottses, meanwhile, ended up with all of Faucett's possessions, including the gold in his pocket and the deed to his ranch. Not surprisingly, the local sheriff suspected foul play. But when questioned, the couple merely claimed that Faucett had left the house after mentioning something about urgent business on the West Coast. At the time, no body had been found. The Pottses produced a signed receipt for Faucett's ranch; it appeared they'd been given the property legitimately. The sheriff had no grounds to take them in.

Not long after, however, the Pottses decided to move to Rock Springs, Wyoming, and their former home was rented to a couple named Brewer. When Mr. Brewer decided to do a little remodeling and started to dig out the basement, he found a grisly surprise: mangled body parts in a shallow grave. An inquest determined that the body was that of Miles Faucett. The sheriff quickly booked the first train to Rock Springs so he could arrest the Pottses for murder.

Once cornered, the Pottses told a complex story. The couple claimed that Faucett had killed himself in their home; they said they were afraid no one would believe them, so they tried to cover it up. Elizabeth said she had caught Faucett raping their daughter Edith. When Faucett came to collect on their debt, they confronted him. Instead of collecting the money the couple owed him, Faucett decided to give the family every-thing he owned—the deed to his ranch, cash, and other items—to try and make up for his egregious crime. In return for all of his possessions, he asked the Potts to stay mum and agree not to turn him in to law officials. The pair capitulated. They had all been drinking, however, and Faucett became increasingly despondent over what he'd done. With the couple looking on, he suddenly took out his pistol and shot himself in the head.

The Pottses said they'd done some fast, if not wrong-headed, think-ing. Josiah took the body to the basement and buried it. On the train ride in police custody from Rock Springs to Carlin, he also nervously confessed that he cut up the corpse with an ax; he then chopped the remains into smaller pieces so he could burn them. The stench, however, was awful; he abandoned the plan and reburied what was left. While they both confessed to covering up the death, they both proclaimed their innocence. Neither would ever admit to murdering the man.

The couple's story did not convince the police. The suicide excuse seemed a little too convenient. It did not completely explain the man-gled, rotting body parts or the signed deed for Faucett's property, which may have been a forgery. The authorities might have let mild-mannered Josiah take all the blame for the crime, but Elizabeth's domineering personality made them conclude that the killing was actually her idea. Even if Elizabeth didn't pull the trigger or try to get rid of the body, she controlled Josiah's every move, they believed. The crime, moreover, was so heinous, it seemed to beg for a double death penalty.

Not all agreed. Some Nevadans felt strongly that it was wrong to hang a woman, and they sent a petition to the state Board of Pardons asking that the sentence for Elizabeth be changed to life in prison. But their petition was denied.

Still, questions about the crime persisted, even after the hanging. Was it possible, some wondered, that Faucett had incriminating evidence about the Pottses—and perhaps was blackmailing them? Maybe there was more to the matter than just a conflict over cash? A reporter dug into the case to see if he could unravel the mystery, but the information he uncovered was even more confounding.

According to an unnamed reporter who published his story in the *San Francisco Examiner* on March 29, 1887, Elizabeth wasn't just married to Josiah; she was also married to, you guessed it, Miles Faucett. During the time that she and Josiah were separated, Elizabeth had traveled west and wed Faucett in Fresno, California—an act of bigamy. Faucett, a carpenter by trade, had apparently paid a marriage consultant $105—a sizeable fee in those days—to arrange the union. Later, when he found out that Elizabeth was still married, he demanded that Elizabeth pay him back. Instead, Elizabeth apparently took off and went back to Josiah.

Faucett followed her to Nevada and—oddly enough—took a room with the Pottses before he purchased his ranch. The details aren't clear. How a husband and wife could live under the same roof with another "husband" the wife had fraudulently married seems more than odd. One wonders what kind of arrangement, if any, Elizabeth had with Faucett, and if Josiah was privy to what had happened in Fresno. We just don't know.

The questions remain to this day. It may be that Faucett had something to hang over the couple because Elizabeth owed him money for the consultant fee. Perhaps he threatened to expose Elizabeth as a bigamist if the couple didn't pay him the $105. And no one can say if the Pottses' claim that Faucett raped their daughter was true or not. Everyone in town knew he lived at the couple's home, so the accusation could potentially have been devastating. Men were strung up for less.

Even today, however, the case still troubles historians. Was Elizabeth really the driving force behind the grisly murder? Did she live a secret life? She may have been a dominating and bloodthirsty woman, or she may have been a luckless soul, trapped between two men in a fateful triangle. And no one came out alive. ⇥

CHAPTER SEVEN

ELLEN WATSON

The FIRST Woman Hanged in Wyoming

If we read the newspaper stories of her day or the legends that have passed into western history, we might conclude that the woman known as Cattle Kate was little more than an opportunist, a two-bit rustler, and a prostitute. We are supposed to believe that she was so desperate to build up her cattle herd that she would do anything for a buck—or a beef cow. It didn't matter if the ownership of the animal was questionable. For years, Cattle Kate had been tried by the press and public opinion. History has not been kind to her.

However, if we look a little closer, we find that Cattle Kate may not have been the pariah of Wyoming as we have been led to believe. It appears Cattle Kate was really a victim of greed—not her own but that of the large ranching interests.

Cattle Kate, of course, wasn't her real name. This was a dubious title bestowed upon her by the press to vilify and convict her in the court of public opinion. Cattle Kate's real name was Ellen Liddy Watson. She was born in Ontario, Canada, on July 2, 1860. In 1877, her father moved his young family to Smith County, Kansas, to settle on free government land.

Ellen Watson on one of her favorite horses. Watson was lynched in 1889 by a group of vigilantes who wanted her land. She was the first and last woman hanged in Wyoming. DENVER PUBLIC LIBRARY, WESTERN HISTORY COLLECTION, F-21182.

In 1879 Ellen fell in love with a nearby farmer named William Pickell. The couple married in November. Pickell was a heavy drinker, and it wasn't long before he started to beat his young wife. At one point, he is reported to have taken a whip to her. By 1883, Ellen had taken all the physical abuse she could stand. She stayed with her parents while she recovered, then she worked as a cook and a domestic. On February 14, 1884, she filed for a divorce in Red Cloud, Nebraska, which was only a few miles from her parents' home.

While she waited for her divorce, she worked in Colorado and Wyoming, mostly as a cook. While she was living in Rawlins, Wyoming, in the winter of 1886, she met an attractive man named James Averell. The interest was mutual. Averell had a general store/café/bar on the Oregon Trail near the Sweetwater River. He asked her if she'd like to come and cook in his café. He told her she could charge half a dollar a meal and keep what she charged. James Averell was an enterprising young man who also had other business concerns, including a spread on the Sweetwater River that was good bottomland. Ellen Watson was interested in the business deal—and in being closer to Averell.

Her divorce was finalized, and her new relationship with Averell blossomed. In May of 1886 the young couple got in his freight wagon and drove to Lander, Wyoming, where they filled out a marriage application and had it notarized. There is no record of them actually getting married, but many historians assume that they did. It's likely they married far from home so no one would know. The couple would be able to get more land through the Homestead Act if they were unmarried and filed separately for homesteading claims.

Ellen filed on the land next to Averell's at the Cheyenne Land Office on March 23, 1888. This move gave the couple 320 acres. A clever move. Between them they owned all the water rights between the Sweetwater River and Horse Creek. Their future looked bright, indeed. In June of 1888, Averell was named postmaster and justice of the peace. A house was constructed, and Ellen Watson (she did not take Averell's name) moved onto her newly acquired land. She took to ranching, buying stock from emigrants on the nearby Oregon Trail and Military Road. She also cooked at the café, putting her money into their ranches. The couple built barns, fences, corrals, and obtained a brand.

But there was a problem. Both James Averell and Ellen Watson were about to step on the toes of a few large ranchers who did not take kindly to interlopers. Watson and Averell had what these ranchers wanted. In the summer of 1889, the ranchers decided to act.

Ellen Watson and her fourteen-year-old ranch hand, John DeCory, were returning home from visiting a tribe of Shoshone Indians by the Sweetwater River not far from her ranch. She had just purchased a fancy pair of buckskin moccasins. There was no way for Ellen Watson to know that she would not live to see the warm July sunset that evening. As she

Vigilantes hanged Watson's husband, Jim Averell, alongside her near the Sweetwater River. #088, AMERICAN HERITAGE CENTER, UNIVERSITY OF WYOMING.

walked up to her cabin, anticipating a cool drink of water, she noticed her fence had been ripped down and her cattle driven off. Before she knew it, she was greeted by six angry ranchers, who accused her of rustling. Besides John DeCory, her step-nephew Ralph Cole was also a firsthand witness to what happened next.

Rancher Albert Bothwell was the primary accuser, joined by vigilante ranchers John Durbin, Ernest Mclean, Robert Calbraith, Robert Conner, and Tom Sun. One of the men had driven his wagon up to the cabin, and Bothwell grabbed Watson and threw her in the back. Watson protested; she told the men she had purchased, not stolen, her cattle and that they knew it. She argued that she'd had these cattle for a year. But her pleas of innocence were in vain.

Shortly after the kidnapping, Frank Buchanan, a close family friend, rode up to the ranch house for a visit. DeCory filled him in on what had just happened. Hoping he could be of help, Buchanan took off after the mob at a gallop.

Averell, in the meantime, was on his way to Casper and crossed paths with the vigilantes en route. The men shouted that they had a warrant for his arrest. Averell asked to see the warrant. "This warrant is enough for you," one cattleman reportedly replied, pointing his gun at Averell.

Averell was also tossed into the back of the buckboard with his frightened wife. The mob drove toward the Sweetwater River, not far from present-day Independence Rock. They drove into a rocky wash and headed for a handy pine with a straight branch; the men quickly tossed two ropes over the limb. Hanging a man was one thing, but hanging a woman was dirtier work than any had done before, and they wanted to get it over with quickly—and away from prying eyes. The mob forced the pair to stand on a high rock and looped nooses over their heads.

Trouble was, no one in the mob was practiced in the gruesome art of lynching. Their victims' legs and arms were not bound, the drop from the rock wasn't quite high enough to get the job done properly, and the victims' ropes were placed too close together on the tree limb. Buchanan galloped up and saw the nooses on Watson and Averell. Hoping to save his friends, he shot John Durbin in the hip. More shots rang out. In the chaos, Bothwell pushed Averell off the rock, then Watson.

The drop, however, was not far enough to break the couple's necks. The condemned pair kicked their legs hopelessly, and they frantically grabbed at the ropes above their heads, trying to relieve the pressure as the nooses cinched tighter and tighter. They suffocated by degrees. In the struggle, Ellen kicked off her new buckskin moccasins. Finally, the choking sounds ended.

Frank Buchanan, meanwhile, had ridden off to find the sheriff. Deputy Sheriff Watson formed a small posse and brought along Dr. Joseph Benson, the coroner. They arrived at the killing field at 2:00 A.M. the next day. Reportedly, the lawmen rode over to the victims and cut them down. Later, they interviewed the boys who had witnessed Watson's kidnapping and also took Buchanan's testimony.

Ellen Watson and James Averell were buried unceremoniously in a common grave.

Sheriff Watson interviewed the vigilantes, all six of whom admitted to the lynching. Perhaps they thought it wouldn't be a problem; hanging a male rustler, after all, was something the law often forgave. The six cattlemen were, moreover, respected ranchers and businessmen, members of the powerful Wyoming Stock Growers Association (WSGA). What they didn't realize, though, was that hanging a woman—no matter her crime—was almost unthinkable to most in the West. Each of vigilantes was required to post a $5,000 bond, a hefty sum in that day.

The WSGA immediately went to the defense of the six killers. In the association's view, rustling was an offense that required the stiffest penalty—with or without legal sanction. If the six men were convicted, the association argued it would send the wrong message and encourage cattle rustling. Not surprisingly, local papers agreed. Wyoming's *Daily Sun* and *Daily Leader* both came down squarely on the side of the major cattle interests. A July 23, 1889, editorial in the *Daily Sun* read: "This heroic treatment [The hanging of a woman "rustler"] must prevail and the gentlemen who have resorted to it are entitled to the support and sympathy of all good citizens."

On the same day, the *Daily Sun* posted an inflammatory article that described Watson as a prostitute who went by the name Kate Maxwell— "Cattle Kate," the newspaper called her. The *Sun* ran a retraction of sorts the next day, but the damage was done. Public opinion had turned in favor of the large ranchers.

On August 25, 1889, the six lynchers appeared before a grand jury, which would weigh the evidence and determine if they would be charged with a crime. None of the key prosecution witnesses was able to testify. Frank Buchanan, who had risked his life to save his friends, did not appear. His life had been threatened, so authorities jailed him in Cheyenne, Wyoming, for his own protection. His friends were able to get him released from protective custody; but fearing for his life, Buchanan immediately cleared out of Carbon County, Wyoming, vowing never to return. Ralph Cole, another valuable witness, died of what many suspected was poisoning before he could testify. His death was officially listed as "mountain fever." John DeCory, fearing for his life, fled to Steamboat Springs, Colorado. He sent a letter to the *Casper Weekly Mail* in August of 1889 stating, "She [Watson] bought them [cattle] and paid her own money for them and had them in her possession ever since I'd been with her." Even a stock detective for the WSGA, George Henderson, was found with a bullet hole in his head. Henderson had been gathering evidence against Watson and Averell, but perhaps he'd discovered evidence that implicated the vigilantes instead.

Without witnesses, the prosecution had no case, and the grand jury had no choice; it let the six cattlemen go free.

The acting prosecuting attorney called for a second inquest, perhaps hoping that others in the area would come forward and testify. But fear of reprisals was all too real.

Watson should have prospered in Wyoming. She had a good eye for land and cattle ranching, and she had filed a claim on one of the nicest sections of ground on the Sweetwater River. There was excellent grazing on her land, and, just as critical, the grass was so rich it could be cut and the hay stored for use during the harsh winters.

In Albert Bothwell's mind, however, he had the right to ruin her name and take her life. More than 100 years later, at least one of those things can be remedied. ⇥

OUTLAW MOLLS

STANDING BY
HER
BAD MAN

SOME OF THE WOMEN IN THESE CHAPTERS WERE not bad people per se, but their taste in men was questionable. If you hung around with robbers and murderers in the Old West, you ran the risk of being labeled a criminal; by association you were guilty. Sometimes, however, a woman didn't have to do anything at all to gain outlaw status. Instead, some writer made up a fantastic outlaw biography, a love story even, because it helped sell books (and, later, motion pictures). Before the woman knew it, the legend had spread like prairie fire. She was infamous.

The lovely Rose of Cimarron was just such a case. She was a made-up heroine who allegedly fell for a famous member of the Doolin Gang, one of the most well-known outlaw bands of the day. If Rose's story were true, it would be one of the great outlaw love tales of all time.

The tales spun about Belle Starr are just as outlandish, but at least Belle was a dyed-in-the-wool, documented horse thief who did some jail time. In real life, she stood by her men—at least for a while. Belle's boyfriends were thieves or serious criminals. They mostly ended up shot or hanged.

Laura Bullion was caught and arrested with her man, the Tall Texan, Ben Kilpatrick, because they'd carelessly spent their stolen money, and officials followed the paper trail. Annie Rogers, the lover of the famous but brutal Kid Curry (aka Harvey Logan), was caught trying to cash stolen notes. Etta Place took off for South America with Butch Cassidy and the Sundance Kid. Teenagers Jennie Stevens and Anna McDoulet wanted to be associated with the Doolin Gang. They had puppy-love interests in several gang members but were written off as youngsters until they started to bootleg, rustle cattle, and move stolen goods.

It has always been a risky business to set your cap for an out-law—as the women in this chapter learned the hard way. ✛

CHAPTER EIGHT

THE ROSE OF CIMARRON

Common Country Girl OR Epic Heroine?

In real life, the Rose of Cimarron was a woman named Rose Dunn. In song and story, she was a famous outlaw. In truth, she was no more an outlaw than the average schoolteacher.

Dunn lived in northern Oklahoma by the Cimarron Strip and was a contemporary of fellow Oklahomans Cattle Annie, Little Britches, and the Doolin Gang. Her story was told and retold; she was portrayed in books, news stories, dime novels, and even in a silent movie. According to the myth, she was one of the prettiest girls in the state, with a smile and a figure to die for. Cowboys would ride all night just to watch her walk down the boardwalk. Any young buck in the county would be willing to shoot it out to gain her favor, but—as the stories went—Rose was in love with an outlaw named "Bitter Creek" George Newcomb, from the Doolin Gang. She could shoot, ride, and rope better than any ten cowboys, so the gang let her join them on outlaw adventures, and soon she was stealing cows from Kansas to Texas.

Enter reality. The real Rose Dunn was born in Cowley, Kansas, on September 5, 1878. She was good looking, with chocolate eyes, thick dark hair, and a lovely complexion, but she probably wasn't the best catch in Pawnee County, let alone the state. She had a good education from a Catholic school. When her father died, her mother married a physician named Call. She had some trouble accepting her stepfather, and the two would clash now and then. Whenever this happened, Rose would go and stay for a few days at the ranch of her older brother Dee.

Dee had some shady cattle dealings with the Doolin Gang. Before they started robbing banks and trains, the gang rustled livestock, and Dee would fence the stolen beef. Big brother also let the boys hang out on his ranch when things got hot and they needed a place to hide. Rose likely had met the gang in passing, or knew a few by name.

Many of the stories about Rose say she was arrested for various crimes. The truth is, there is no record of her being arrested or even questioned. Ironically, the Rose of Cimarron legend didn't begin until the Doolin Gang were all dead. The stories didn't start to circulate until more than a decade after the events they detailed had passed. By this time, the real Rose was middle-aged, married, and a mother.

In 1898, at approximately nineteen years of age, the real Rose Dunn wed a blacksmith and well digger named Charles Nobel. They remained married until Nobel's death in 1932, at which point Rose was about fifty-three. She later married a man named Richard Fleming. The other details of her life are sketchy. Fact and fiction got entwined over the years, making it increasingly thorny to separate the two.

The legend went something like this: The Rose of Cimarron, named for the Cimarron Strip in Oklahoma, was a drop-dead beauty. She fell deeply and tragically in love with a dashing Doolin Gang outlaw named Bitter Creek. He got his nickname because of a cowboy song he liked to sing, "I'm a wolf from Bitter Creek/It's my night to howl." On a bright September morning in 1893, she decided to visit him at one of the gang's hideouts, Mrs. Pierre's Boarding House and Livery in Ingalls, Oklahoma, just a few miles from Dunn's home. The upper floor served as a sleeping area. The lower half of her establishment was a restaurant of sorts—a place for men to cut the dust after being on the trail. The Doolin Gang liked Ingalls because the town was off the beaten path and they were less likely to be disturbed.

At some point during this fateful autumn morning, Rose looked out the window and saw a bunch of deputies trying to sneak up and ambush her beloved Bitter Creek and the rest of the Doolin Gang. She watched from the upstairs window as the posse circled the house. Bitter Creek saw the deputies, too, and he started blasting his six-gun to warn his friends and take out the lawmen. Knowing her love might need medical attention—or at the very least would soon run out of bullets—she strapped on a Colt and grabbed a handy rifle and a box of shells. Climbing down a ladder from the boarding house to the livery, she ran into the street, braving the gunfire. Rose counted on the chivalry of the deputies, whom she figured would not dare shoot a woman. Her skirt flew as she raced to her lover's side.

She made it over to Bitter Creek as he was shooting his last rounds and handed him her pistol, cartridge belts, and rifle. He had been shot, and she was desperately worried that he had a mortal wound. By this time, the rest of the gang was shooting at the posse, too. When it was over, as many as twelve people were dead. Bitter Creek was badly wounded, but Rose managed to get him to safety, where she could nurse his wounds. Her womanly touch made the difference; he pulled through. Not long after his recovery, however, he ran into more trouble at Dee's ranch.

As legend has it, Dee—a coward and a traitor—was under pressure from the law to turn in his gangster friends, and he was eager to collect the reward money on Bitter Creek's head. Betraying his sister and her chance of future happiness, he shot Bitter Creek dead. Rose vowed never to speak to Dee again.

Was she doomed to misery? Apparently not. In folklore's tidy endings, Rose was able to love again—this time a prominent man in the county. It is said they lived happily ever after.

If this all sounds like a silly Old West novel or a grade-C western movie, you're not alone. But if you consider the different twists that have been added over the years, the story gets even better. Some recount the tale of the exquisite Rose of Cimarron and her exploits after Bitter Creek takes that final bullet. In these versions, the full-busted Oklahoma lass marries a politician, or one of the lawmen who chased the Doolin Gang. Some tales have her marrying a poor, but honest farmer.

*For years, many believed this was a photo of Rose Dunn, the "Rose of Cimarron."
However, the woman pictured is actually a prisoner of the local jail; a lawman asked
her to pose for the image in exchange for a reduced jail sentence, so he could use the
photo in a story he'd written about the legendary Rose of Cimarron.*

Whatever the tall tale may be, the picture we so often see of Rose—showing a young beauty wearing a six-shooter and sporting a floppy hat—was completely staged and fabricated. The woman in the photograph isn't the real Rose Dunn; the woman in the image is an unknown prisoner at the local jail in Guthrie, Oklahoma, who dressed up with the hat and gun and pretended to be Rose in exchange for reduced jail time. A local lawman asked her to do it in order to help him sell a story he'd written about Rose.

The Rose of fiction was a star-crossed maiden who fell in love with an outlaw and became one, too. It was a romance story too good to die.

The real Rose Dunn, however, wasn't even in Ingalls at the time of the famous shoot-out. She was at her brother's ranch.

"Bitter Creek" George Newcomb was a real person who rode with the Doolin Gang, and he did meet his end on Dee's ranch, along with his outlaw partner "Black Face" Charlie Pierce, on July 1, 1895. Apparently, Dee owed Bitter Creek some money, and the outlaw had come to collect—but Dee paid in lead, not gold.

Making up tall tales about the frontier was a western tradition, a source of entertainment. But it appears that the saga of Rose Dunn, the Rose of Cimarron, was an orchestrated, manufactured western fairy tale. ⊷

CHAPTER NINE

BELLE STARR
Not Quite the
BANDIT QUEEN

Myra Maybelle Shirley, better known as Belle Starr, was not the "Queen of the Bandits," the "Queen of the Outlaws," or the "Petticoat Terror of the Plains," as newspapers or dime novels proclaimed. Nor was she a misunderstood heroine, a Robin Hood bandit, or a gun-slinging member of an outlaw gang.

Belle Starr was, however, a woman of paradoxes. She was well educated and was versed in classical literature and music. She knew and loved horses and was a gifted rider from her youth. Starr was also knowledgeable in firearms and was a good shot with both rifle and handgun. As a single mother, she worked hard to feed her two children in trying circumstances. She was a loyal friend and a devoted daughter and sister. She was a petty thief and she willingly harbored dangerous fugitives. Always in need of a new man in her life, Starr was a promiscuous and unfaithful partner. Not known for her beauty, one observer commented that Belle Starr was "hatchet faced" and "flat chested, with a mean mouth."

Playing into the hype that had been written about her, Starr once told a Dallas reporter, "I am a friend to any brave and gallant outlaw."

This famous shot of Belle Starr shows just how she wanted to be remembered: astride her favorite horse and with a six-gun at her side.
RESEARCH DIVISION OF THE OKLAHOMA HISTORICAL SOCIETY, #1356.

She had been characterized as a woman who rode a tall, handsome horse with a Colt .45 Army revolver on her side. The papers declared that she robbed from the rich and gave to the poor—that she had a sense of fair play. Thanks mostly to the *National Police Gazette* and other sensational publications that printed scores of stories about Starr in the late 1870s and 1880s, her legend became a national phenomenon in her own lifetime.

Belle Starr was launched into public awareness in 1876 at the trial of the Younger Brothers (she was then known as Belle Shirley). She had kept company with the outlaws, and her name was mentioned time and again at the lengthy trial and noted by reporters who crowded the proceedings. Her association with so many famous bandits, and her recent trial and jail sentence in 1873 for horse theft, made her newsworthy for a readership starved for any information on an outlaw woman. Like Calamity Jane, Belle simply happened to be in the right place at the right time to catch the spotlight. And like Calamity Jane, Belle's personal life was nothing like her media persona.

Myra Maybelle Shirley was born on February 5, 1848, outside Carthage, Missouri. Her father, John Shirley, was a successful business-man. He had interests in a blacksmith shop, a tavern, an inn, and a store. He also speculated in real estate. Young Myra Maybelle, called Belle by her family, had a fine education at the Carthage Female Academy and was brought up to be a lady. She played the piano, read, and went on long horseback rides with her brothers. Having a bit of the tomboy in her, she liked to shoot and hunt.

Her world of privilege, however, ended with the Civil War. Both Union and Confederate forces occupied Jasper County. The Shirley fam-ily sided with the South. Belle's brother, Bud, rode with Confederate "bushwhackers" (guerrilla fighters) under the direction of "Bloody Bill" Anderson and William Quantrill. He rose to the rank of captain. As a bushwhacker, Bud Shirley was good friends with Jesse and Frank James, as well as Cole Younger and his brothers. On leave or when hiding from Union forces, Bud Shirley would bring home the James and the Younger brothers, who were welcomed at his family table. Belle got to know the James and Younger brothers quite well, and they always held a special place in her heart. As a truly gray Southerner, she always appreciated those who dedicated themselves to the cause.

During the early summer of 1864, Union forces closed in on Bud Shirley and some comrades while they were eating at a Southern sympathizer's home in Missouri. To spare the family any repercussions, the rebels tried to slip into the woods. Shirley took a fatal round going over a fence before he could escape. Belle took his death hard and never stopped blaming the U.S. government for his death. She wanted revenge. For Belle, every time she sidestepped the law or sheltered an outlaw, it was a blow against her brother's killers.

Ruined by the war, the Shirley family liquidated their assets and relocated to Texas, near present-day Dallas. The reversal of fortunes was a bitter cup. John Shirley had been an important man in his community, but now that the war was over, he had lost nearly everything. Since he was a Southerner, he could no longer hold public office, and carpetbaggers thwarted his every turn. He set up a new life for his family, but he never forgot his Confederate roots.

A number of Southerners, especially former bushwhackers, were having a hard time accepting defeat and vowed to keep fighting. The James and Younger brothers were among this group. The pair of brothers felt that robbing banks, holding up trains, and rustling livestock were the best ways to strike back at the Union; and these activities were more profitable and easier than planting corn under the hot sun. They traveled between Missouri, Kansas, Oklahoma, and Texas on their raids. They still sought shelter and a meal from fellow Southerners and were warmly welcomed as freedom fighters who refused to give up. Because of their association with Bud Shirley, when the gang was in Texas, they knew they were always welcomed at the Shirley home.

As the daring exploits of Jesse James and Cole Younger drew media attention (and as a mythology about the gang developed just as exponentially), Belle found herself caught up in the vortex. She was part of James Gang folklore that was promoted by papers, magazines, and dime novels. One of the most persistent myths is that Belle was the young love interest of the outlaw Cole Younger. After robbing a bank in 1866, Cole Younger sought refuge at her home. It was said that the two soon became lovers. Depending on the person telling the story, Younger remained her clandestine lover for some time. Other versions have them getting married. Nevertheless, the product of their union was a daughter named Pearl. To shield Pearl and Belle, the noble Younger disappears, only seeing his lover and daughter occasionally. While there would be other men, it was said they never measured up to Cole Younger.

The only problem is that Younger was not even in the state of Texas when this romance is said to have taken place. Belle liked Younger and admired him as a man and as an outlaw, but they were only friends, never lovers. The story was thought up by a reporter wanting to advance his career.

Another legend has Belle falling in love with a dashing outlaw named Jim Reed, a reckless member of the James/Younger Gang and close friend of Cole Younger. While holding over at the Shirley home, Reed fell for the sassy young woman, they both got a bit carried away, and Belle found herself pregnant. Reed wanted to marry her on the spot, but her folks would not have it. They forbad the couple from seeing each other. Not able to quench his love for Belle, he brought a band of outlaws to the Shirley house at midnight and called for his true love. Belle's father insisted he leave, but an outlaw buddy held a Colt to the old man's head while Jim swung Belle up into the saddle. The lovers found a preacher so Reed could make Belle an honest woman.

The truth, of course, is something quite different. On November 1, 1866, in Collins County, Texas, eighteen-year-old Belle did marry a Jim Reed—a saddle maker. The Reeds and Shirleys had known each other in Missouri. Reed was no outlaw—at least not yet. He was never a member of the James/Younger Gang. He didn't come dashing into the Shirleys' yard, six-gun in hand, and take off with his bride. The couple's marriage was blessed not only by the clergy, but by both of Belle's parents.

At first, the newlyweds stayed with her folks. A little later, they felt they could better their fortunes back in Missouri where Reed's relatives lived. Hoping that things had settled down after the war, the couple went north so Reed could farm his family's land. Reed soon proved that he indeed had wild oats that needed sowing. He wasn't much for working the land and was bored with his family responsibilities. He started to drink and fell in with bad company. He had a few minor skirmishes with the law.

In 1868, Belle gave birth to a daughter whom they named Pearl. Fatherhood did not settle Reed down. His first crimes were petty misdemeanors such as selling whiskey on the indian reservation. Soon he graduated to armed robbery and had a price on his head. Then he killed a man to avenge his brother. With warrants out for his arrest, he was not sure where to turn. By 1869, the situation was very hot, so Reed took his wife and child and headed for California until things cooled down. In California, they had their second child, whom they named James Edwin. Reed drank and gambled and couldn't stay out of trouble. He got involved in a counterfeit money scandal and once again had the law at his heels. He fled California on a fast horse. His family returned to Texas by stage to meet up with him.

By 1873, Reed was implicated in more murders and robberies. Their marriage was strained, and Belle left him, taking their two children with her. Soon after, in 1874, Jim Reed's misdeeds caught up with him. A friend named John Morris double-crossed Reed for the reward money on his head and shot him dead. Legend says that Belle refused to identify her husband's body so Morris could not get the reward.

Widowhood was hard for Belle. She was destitute after Reed was killed. She moved back to Missouri to stay with his parents until she could get established. She tried to raise her children and make ends meet. This part of her life is hard to pin down historically, since there are few records to draw upon. Legend has Belle doing a number of implausible things: running tables as a professional gambler, riding with the James Gang, working as a madam at a whorehouse, and running an inn. Allegedly, she was also charged as a horse thief. Perhaps the strangest legend has Belle in 1878 supposedly breaking into a general store during a fierce storm near Dallas, Texas. Cold, she started a fire in the corner of the building to get warm and make coffee. The fire got out of control and burned the store to the ground. The next day, she was jailed and charged with arson. She borrowed enough money to pay her fine and left. All we know for certain about her during this time is she did what she could to feed her kids.

In 1880, Belle became very interested in a dashing Cherokee outlaw named Sam Starr, five years her junior. They married on June 5, 1880. The couple cleared a farm in Oklahoma Territory, near the Canadian River on Cherokee land. Belle called their home "Younger Bend" in honor of the Younger Gang, whom they both admired. Their remote farm was soon frequented by outlaws and wanted men. In the *Fort Smith Elevator*, Belle Starr wrote the following sketch for reporter John F. Weaver: "My home became famous as an outlaw's ranch long before I was visited by my . . . [James/Younger Gang] friends. Indeed, I never corresponded with any of my old associates . . . Jesse James first came in and remained several weeks. He was unknown to my husband . . . I introduced Jesse as one Mr. Williams from Texas."

In 1882, Belle and Sam Starr were charged with horse theft. They had some of their neighbor's stock mixed in with their own and weren't

Belle Starr called her homestead in Oklahoma Territory "Younger Bend" in honor of family friend, and her favorite outlaw, Cole Younger.

eager to return the animals. To make matters worse, they sold the animals. The pair came before Judge Isaac Parker, the famous "Hanging Judge" in Fort Smith, Arkansas. Both Belle and Starr did jail time for this offense. Sam Starr was given twelve months of hard labor; Belle Starr was given nine months. Judge Parker thought he was being lenient with the pair (and by his standards, he was). This was a first offense for both of them, and he hoped the two rustlers had learned their lesson. Belle was a model prisoner and was released early.

When Sam Starr returned home, he continued to sell whiskey to the Indians (a crime at the time) and trade stolen livestock. He stayed away from home for long periods of time on his outlaw adventures. While he was gone, a lonely Belle occasionally entertained all-night guests. She often spent time with a family friend, a wanted outlaw named John Middleton.

Middleton was being hounded by deputies and decided to leave the area. He drowned in 1885 while attempting a treacherous river crossing. Belle's personal Colt .45 was found on the body.

In January of 1886, Belle was again charged with horse theft and was summoned to Fort Smith, Arkansas. This time she fought the charges.

On May 23, 1886, she officially pleaded not guilty (the trial would be the following September). She visited friends and took a picture with another famous outlaw named "Blue" Duck, who was appealing his death sentence for murder. For some reason, Duck's council thought it would be good press for him to be photographed with the famous Belle Starr. Belle was eager to oblige. She was always happy to grant interviews with reporters and have her picture taken. In no time, the media had a field day. Headlines read that "Queen of the Outlaws" Belle Starr and murderer "Blue" Duck had been clandestine lovers for years. Three months after pleading not guilty, she returned to face her charge. She was acquitted.

At a Christmas party on December 17, 1886, Sam Starr ran into a man he hated, a fellow named Frank West. Each man went for his gun and shot. Both bullets went true, and each man dropped over dead. Belle was a widow again.

Not one to let the December frost form under her feet, within days of Sam's burial, Belle moved in with an outlaw named Jack Spaniard. It seems that Spaniard wasn't fated for a long life either. Within a few months, he was tried and summarily hanged for murder. After fashionably mourning for at least a few days, Belle began living with a Cherokee Indian named Bill July. The two married in 1888; Belle was forty, and July was twenty-four.

The last chapter of Belle's life occured in 1889. July was facing charges of horse theft. Belle rode part of the way to Fort Smith with him, where they stayed with friends. On the morning of February 3, 1889, July headed off to face Judge Parker, and Belle started for home at Younger Bend. Her checkered life was cut short by a blast from a scattergun. She was blown from the saddle of her horse onto the muddy trace. As she tried to get up, she was shot in the face at close range and died instantly. Frightened, her horse bolted. Officials were never able to find her killer.

Most of the newspapers in the country ran stories about the death of this star of dime novels. The 1889 *New York Times* headline read: "A Desperate Woman Killed." The story described her as "the wife of Cole Younger." It seemed her myth was more important than the truth, and Belle Starr's life remains a mix of fact and fiction to this day. →

In 1886 Belle Starr posed for a picture with convicted murderer and outlaw "Blue" Duck. It was rumored the two were lovers, but the truth is that Starr barely knew the famous bandit. RESEARCH DIVISION OF THE OKLAHOMA HISTORICAL SOCIETY, #4631.

Symbols of Starr's life and a poem adorn her grave marker, just outside Porum, Oklahoma. RESEARCH DIVISION OF THE OKLAHOMA HISTORICAL SOCIETY, #1464.1.

CHAPTER TEN

LAURA BULLION
A Flower IN THE Wild Bunch

H er given name was Laura Bullion, but she was also known as the "Rose of the Wild Bunch," "Della Rose," the "Thorny Rose," or simply "Rose." The famous paramour of at least two illustrious members of the Wild Bunch—Will Carver and Ben Kilpatrick—Bullion was the last associate of this group to perish, dying in 1961. Some historians believe she was buried in Memphis, Tennessee, under the name of Freda Bullion Lincoln.

Laura Bullion was born in Knickerbocker, Texas, circa 1876. The southern Texas of her youth was a land where the whiskey flowed freely, changing the brands on the other guy's cattle with a saddle cinch ring was considered an art form, and arguments were often settled by fist, Bowie knife, or Colt. Bullion was a pretty girl who could be a bit high-strung. When she was under pressure, she was an inveterate gum chewer, which seemed to calm her down. She liked pretty things and enjoyed dressing up, but she also enjoyed the outdoors and knew how to take care of herself.

Her father was a known outlaw with a passion for robbing trains. He was considered a bold bandit, if not an unlucky one. On a train robbery in New Mexico, he was shot to death. Laura's widowed mother was hardly a

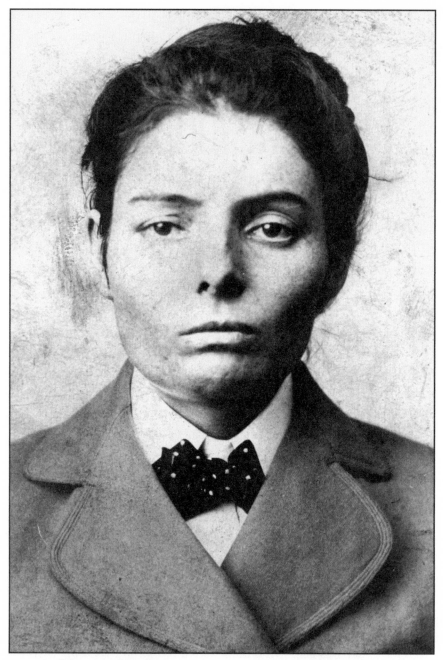

Laura Bullion's mug shot after her 1901 arrest in St. Louis, Missouri.
PINKERTON ARCHIVES.

Between heists, the Wild Bunch visited Fanny Porter's "Hell's Half Acre" for female company. This photo taken in Fort Worth, Texas, shows, left to right, the Sundance Kid, Will Carver, Ben Kilpatrick, Kid Curry, and Butch Cassidy.
DENVER PUBLIC LIBRARY, WESTERN HISTORY COLLECTION, Z-49.

good role model, either. Fereby Bullion was known as the county floozy. More than once, Laura and her brother were abandoned or handed off to Fereby's parents, the Bylers, while Fereby consorted with various boyfriends. By the time Laura was a teenager, she was more than ready to leave home. She had learned some lessons from her mother, though, and she knew what a woman could do to turn a dollar in a cowboy town. But where her mother was an amateur, she would be a professional.

Knickerbocker, Texas, and the surrounding area were the stomping grounds for a fine collection of rustlers and road agents. This part of Texas produced the infamous Ketchum brothers, Tom and Sam, who ran a bloody group of thieves known as the "Black Jack" Ketchum Gang. The area also sprouted two other famous outlaws, Ben the "Tall Texan" Kilpatrick and his close friend William Carver. Both men rode with the Ketchum Gang and later with the Wild Bunch, and both would become Laura Bullion's lovers.

Bullion had met Carver in her youth; he was married to her aunt Vianna. After Vianna passed away, Bullion and Carver became lovers. Carver's lifestyle didn't seem to bother Bullion. Some have suggested that the two married, but this seems unlikely. Jeffery Burton, author of *Tom Ketchum and His Gang*, suggests that Carver never considered Bullion a replacement for his first wife. The settling influence of his first wife was gone and a reckless abandon had taken its place. Both Carver and Bullion were lovers of convenience, but it would be wrong to assume that there was not a great deal of mutual affection between the two. He bought her expensive gifts and treated her to long vacations.

Bullion continued to work as a prostitute in her hometown of Knickerbocker. However, most prostitutes did not stay in one place very long, and Laura Bullion was no exception. She wandered around the West, working for different madams to support herself. She may have traveled as far north as Wyoming. However, Texas always drew her back. Eventually, she found herself at Fanny Porter's upscale brothel in San Antonio, Texas, which would become a favorite hideaway of the Wild Bunch. She became good friends with the madam, Fanny Porter, and another prostitute named Annie Rogers. The establishment was on the corner of Durango and San Saba streets in the red light district. For an underprivileged girl from backwater Texas, the splendor and extravagance of the parlor house must have seemed glamorous. She wore beautiful dresses and ate fine food in an expensively furnished mansion.

In the meantime, Carver and Sam Ketchum had opened up a drinking establishment near Fanny Porter's brothel. He visited Bullion as often as he could. For a while, being a saloon keeper seemed like a good profession, but it proved too tame. He lost interest in pouring drinks and decided to seek his fortune with a Colt six-shooter. Rustling and robbing seemed more exciting. From here on, Carver followed a pattern he would live by, and eventually die by: Ride the outlaw trail, make a big score, live it up in town until the money was gone, then go back to work. He rode for two major gangs and freelanced when he was broke.

Carver and Bullion spent time together whenever he blew into town. Both Bullion and Carver had Fanny Porter to thank for the relationship. Many madams could be brutal; working girls often feared them more than abusive clients. Prostitutes generally were not allowed to form personal attachments with patrons. If a man wanted to take a girl away, he often had to buy out her contract first. Meanwhile, if a girl overstepped the bounds, a madam could throw her out on the street or beat her. But Porter acted more like a camp counselor than a prison guard. She didn't mind if one of her charges wanted to hook up with a customer or take a vacation. She wished her "boarder" well and hoped the girl might find some happiness.

Will Carver was making a name for himself as an outlaw and was a wanted man. He joined up with his old friend Ben Kilpatrick, outlaw-mastermind Butch Cassidy, and famous bandits the Sundance Kid and Kid Curry; this loose collection of outlaws became known as the "Fort Worth Five" or the "Wild Bunch," veterans of some of the most lucrative and successful bank and train robberies in the United States. On November 21, 1900, the Fort Worth Five sat in the Swartz photography studio in Fort Worth and had their portrait taken. This act of vanity would later prove to be their undoing. The Wild Bunch had been careful to remain anonymous. No one had a clue what they looked like.

It's not clear how much true happiness Bullion found with Carver. Around 1900, their romantic relationship cooled, although they remained good friends. It appears that Carver had fallen for one of Bullion's colleagues, a prostitute named Callie May Hunt. But Bullion's eye, too, had wandered. She began to favor another member of the Wild Bunch, Ben Kilpatrick, whom she had also known in Knickerbocker, Texas.

Kilpatrick was Bullion's second outlaw lover and the love of her life. Born in Concho County, Texas, in 1877, he was not known as the "Tall Texan" by accident; well over six feet, he towered over his associates. Kilpatrick was known as an easy-going, likeable guy. He had never learned to read, and he was self-conscious about it. He'd study a menu in a restaurant and always order ham and beans, pretending he could read. He was a cheerful man, not moody or withdrawn like Carver. Kilpatrick was known as a top cowhand and a man who could handle himself in a difficult situation. He and Bullion settled into the same sort of "whore and outlaw" relationship she'd had with Carver, but their feelings grew deeper. She loved him enough to follow him on the "Owl Hoot" trail—

Ben Kilpatrick, the "Tall Texan," was a member of the Wild Bunch and the love of Laura Bullion's life. SPECIAL COLLECTIONS DEPAERTMENT, J. WILLARD MARRIOTT LIBRARY, UNIVERSITY OF UTAH.

and was his companion thereafter. Like Carver, the Tall Texan gave Laura Bullion expensive gifts and took her on classy vacations. They would travel as a regular married couple on holiday.

But by 1901, high living had left the couple broke. The Wild Bunch was planning another heist, and this time there seemed to be a place for Bullion, who had proven she could shoot and ride well.

Some historians have suggested that on July 3, 1901, Laura Bullion helped Kilpatrick and Kid Curry—the only members of the Wild Bunch left in the country—hold up the Great Northern Railway Coast Flyer No. 3 near Wagner, Montana. One of the outlaws—it's unknown which one—boarded the train, made his way to the front, and stuck his Colt to the engineer's head, demanding he stop the train. The engineer was ordered to pull the engine and passenger cars away from the express car. The outlaws then used charges of black powder and dynamite to break into the express car and crack the safe. They blew the car to bits, but they managed to get away with perhaps $41,000 in unsigned bank notes. After the robbery, the bandits scattered.

It's evident that Laura Bullion was a participant in this crime, but she did not wield a six-gun and hold up passengers as some have speculated. She stayed with the mounts—an important job when one is escaping by horseback, even if it holds little glamour.

Butch Cassidy and the Sundance Kid were conspicuously absent from this caper; these two most famous members of the Wild Bunch had set sail on February 2, 1901, for South America. They felt the United States had become too "hot" for further outlaw activity. Will Carver had been shot to death earlier that spring in Sonora, Texas, by local authorities.

This robbery by the remaining Wild Bunch outlaws and Bullion proved to be their undoing. By Cassidy's standards, the caper was poorly executed and lacked the master outlaw's meticulous planning.

With their photos in circulation, it was difficult for the outlaws to find a safe haven. They decided the best thing to do was divide the money and split up.

Law enforcement was getting better at tracking stolen money. Not understanding the newfangled techniques, Kilpatrick and Bullion left a paper trail a blind man could follow.

The lovebird outlaws were on a long, lavish vacation, traveling under the name of Mr. and Mrs. Benjamin Arnold. They didn't know their vacation was just about over. In St. Louis, Missouri, the law closed in. The fact that their bags were not packed indicates that the arrest was probably a complete surprise. Scholars debate the exact date of their arrests. Many believe the Tall Texan was picked up on November 5, 1901, while Bullion was apprehended the next morning when she tried to slip out of town. Noted Wild Bunch scholar Dan Buck, however, argues the arrest took place earlier.

The couple pleaded guilty on December 12, 1901. Because there was no women's facility in the area, Bullion was sentenced to five years in a Massachusetts women's prison. While she was locked up, Kilpatrick was moved from a prison in Ohio to Atlanta, Georgia. After she was released on September 19, 1905, a year early, she moved to Atlanta in order to be closer to Kilpatrick. He was released on good behavior in 1911.

It is not known if the star-crossed lovers met up after his release. The romantic in each of us would like to think they did. What is known is that in Sanderson, Texas, the Tall Texan took a fatal bullet in a botched robbery attempt on the Southern Pacific Railroad on March 13, 1912.

What happened to Laura Bullion is lost to history. ⇥

CHAPTER ELEVEN

ANNIE ROGERS
The Bawdy Woman
☙ the Bad Guy

nnie Rogers associated with some of most infamous train and bank
robbers in western history—the Wild Bunch. She was one of the
most attractive and colorful outlaw consorts in the last days of the
Old West. A wanted woman, she was certainly guilty of aiding and abetting, eagerly spending as much of the outlaws' ill-gotten gains as she
could. Nevertheless, she didn't have the soul of a criminal.

Annie Rogers was a well-read, intelligent, attractive, and easy-going
woman. She worked for infamous madam Fanny Porter as a high-end
parlor girl in an upscale brothel in San Antonio, Texas. Porter's house was
in a part of town known as "Hell's Half Acre," but its customers spent
heavenly amounts of money. Members of the Wild Bunch were some of
Rogers' best clients.

Not a lot is known about Rogers' early life, but it's believed she was
born and raised in Texas. Her given name is thought to have been Delia
Moore. (Like most working girls, she almost certainly changed her name
to protect her family.) She married when she was eighteen, but the
relationship was not a good one. Rogers escaped her husband and found
herself in San Antonio, Texas—broke and needing a job. She was hired
by Fanny Porter.

Annie Rogers, a prostitute at Fanny Porter's brothel in San Antonio, Texas, and Kid Curry (Harvey Logan), a cold-blooded killer and member of the Wild Bunch. The two fell in love and traveled around the country together on extravagant vacations.
LIBRARY OF CONGRESS, PRINTS AND PHOTOGRAPHS DIVISION, LC-DIG-PPMSCA-07624.

The Wild Bunch had lots of stolen money to spend and liked to call Porter's whorehouse their home. Members of this gang, and other wanted men, could dull their minds on the expensive wine and enjoy carnal pleasures without fear of legal interference. Porter was a loyal friend to the bandits. She refused to sell out her clients and never buckled when grilled by detectives and deputies.

When Rogers first met Kid Curry, the 145-pound outlaw was spending time with another "soiled dove" on the Porter payroll, Lille Davis. It wasn't long before Rogers was able to win the Kid's heart. Neither gave up their day jobs—or perhaps night jobs would be a more accurate description. When Curry was between heists, the couple took luxurious vacations together, registering as Mr. and Mrs. Curry and living in grand style, staying in the finest hotels and eating expensive meals.

Rogers had chosen to be in the company of quite a violent man. Kid Curry was not only a wanted bank and train robber, he was also a cold-blooded killer. He was responsible for shooting at least nine men. In a little over a month, he had gunned down five men in three separate shootings.

One particular killing spree took place in 1901. In May, Curry found out that one of his best friends, "Flat Nose" Curry, had been shot and killed by Sheriff Jesse Taylor in Utah. A few weeks later, Kid Curry hunted the sheriff down and killed him. Only weeks after that, Curry was involved in a July 3, 1901, train robbery near Wagner, Montana. The gang got away with approximately $41,000. Instead of hightailing it to a hideout, as the other outlaws did, Kid Curry remained; he had a score to settle. Five years earlier, a Montana man named Jim Winters had shot Kid Curry's brother. In the dead of night on July 26, 1901, he snuck onto the Winters ranch, got within rifle range of the lonely ranch house, and waited for sunrise. When Winters stepped outside with a cup of coffee in his hand, Kid Curry picked him off. His revenge completed, Kid Curry got on his horse and headed south to meet up with Rogers for a long vacation.

Rogers managed to find and bring out the gentleman in the brutal Kid Curry. He was generous and devoted to her. To him, she wasn't just some common prostitute he took on vacation; she was someone special. She must have represented the culture, gentility, and stability that his brigand life lacked.

But stability was not in the cards for this couple. On October 26, 1901, a well-dressed Annie Rogers walked into the Fourth National Bank of Nashville and handed a teller a stack of large bills a half inch deep. Suspicious about the number of bills, he consulted a list of serial numbers from stolen bills. He quickly called the police and walked back to his station; he told the pretty lady that her money was being processed. While the two chatted, several police detectives confirmed that the bills were from the infamous July 3 Montana train robbery. The police rushed to the bank and arrested Rogers.

On June 16, 1902, Annie Rogers was brought before Judge Hart to be tried for aiding and abetting in disposing of stolen money and harboring a fugitive. Rogers testified that she had no knowledge that the bills she tried to change had been stolen. She also claimed that she had never seen Curry sign the bills. She further added that the arresting officers had abused her. The prosecution presented a number of witnesses, but what helped Rogers' case was a thirty-five-page deposition from Curry stating that Rogers knew nothing about the money being stolen or where it had come from. He stated that he had given her the money to spend, and did so often. He also admitted that he was a member of the so-called Wild Bunch.

On June 18, 1902, jurors deliberated for less than three hours before returning with a verdict of not guilty. Harvey Logan—Kid Curry—was sentenced to 130 years for his role in the train robbery.

After her acquittal, Rogers returned to Texas. She wrote Kid Curry letters but likely never saw her true love again.

Curry, meanwhile, managed to escape from prison and quickly returned to his old line of work. In a botched robbery in 1904 in Glenwood Springs, Colorado, Curry was fatally wounded. Instead of trying to run, he told his men to take off and that he'd head off the law. After his friends got away, he allegedly shot himself.

Why didn't Kid Curry come back for Rogers after he broke out of prison? It's likely that the lovers both knew that Rogers would be watched by lawmen, and Curry would be nabbed if he tried to see her again. Perhaps they did meet and no one knew about it. Did Rogers resume her profession and go back to Fanny Porter's? Did she marry and settle into a quiet life in a small Texas town? There are more questions than answers. With the death of Kid Curry, Annie Rogers faded into western history. ⇥

CHAPTER TWELVE

ETTA PLACE
The Enigma ⚔ Sundance's Girl

W ho was the real Etta Place? Little is known about her. Her fellow travelers in the Wild Bunch—an infamous gang that included Butch Cassidy and the Sundance Kid—were shy and elusive. Unlike many of the criminal gangs in their day, Butch Cassidy and his associates shunned the media and kept a low profile. Even more mysterious were their lovely female consorts, especially when it came to Place, the most famous Wild Bunch woman. We know she was the long-time companion of Wild Bunch outlaw Harry Longabaugh, the infamous Sundance Kid. She traveled with him to New York, and, along with the Wild Bunch mastermind, Butch Cassidy, the trio sailed for South America in 1901 to start a new life away from bounty hunters, posses, and the Pinkerton Detective Agency.

By 1900, Butch Cassidy and the Sundance Kid were among the most wanted men in the United States and the subject of a national and international manhunt. In light of the Wild Bunch's extraordinary success at robbing banks and trains, and the folklore that such activities generated, it was only natural that interest in Sundance's charming female companion would become more than a passing curiosity. By association, if not by action, Place became a woman of interest, as well as a wanted outlaw.

We know from the only photo of her in existence and from first-hand accounts that Place was an attractive woman with long dark-brown hair and intelligent blue-gray eyes. Indeed, most considered her the best looking of the Wild Bunch women. According to the 1906 Pinkerton Detective Agency files, she was born circa 1879, was five feet five inches tall, 110 to 115 pounds, of medium build, and wore her dark hair high on her head. As Wild Bunch researchers Daniel Buck and Anne Meadows have suggested, the description in the Pinkerton file was from notes made by hospital clinic officials who treated the Sundance Kid and Etta Place for what is believed to have been venereal disease before they sailed for South America.

Before fleeing the country, Sundance took Place to Pennsylvania to visit his relatives. He told his kin that she was his wife. The pair also spent time with his sister, whom he was close to.

The couple traveled to Niagara Falls, then headed to New York City to meet up with Butch Cassidy to prepare to leave the country. The three stayed in a boarding house on Twelfth Street. Etta received a watch, probably bought by Butch Cassidy at the exclusive jeweler Tiffany and Co. The trio had a grand time in the Big Apple, eating, drinking, and seeing shows. They lived it up with their ill-gotten gain. On February 2, 1901, they set sail on the S. S. *Herminius* for Argentina.

It doesn't appear that Place picked up a gun or committed a violent crime when she was associated with the Wild Bunch in the United States, although she might have been more involved than we know. She didn't mind helping the boys spend their loot, so she was certainly an accessory after the fact and privy to what they were doing. And apparently, it didn't seem to bother her that the man, or men, in her life robbed people with Colt .45 revolvers, hammers drawn, threatening to shoot if the loot wasn't handed over.

Few women in nineteenth-century lore are more shadowy than Place. Historians still don't have answers to some of the most fundamental questions about her. What was her real name and where was she born? Where did she grow up? How much schooling did she have? Was she a schoolteacher, a housewife, a chambermaid, a prostitute? Did she marry the Sundance Kid, or did she simply live with him? What was her role in the crimes committed by the outlaw duo in South America? When and why did she come back to the United States—and did the Sundance Kid come with her? Did she go back to South America? Where and when did she die? No one really knows.

As I suggest in my book *Wild Bunch Women*, it seems modern-day history buffs have a thirst to learn more about this Wild Bunch moll, even if the historical well is mostly dry. The more we learn about Place, the more our interest is piqued. A number of historians have spent years researching her, only to come up empty-handed. There were lots of "Place sightings" in the nineteenth century, for example, but most can't be verified.

A case in point: Some have hypothesized that Place left the Sundance Kid in South America and came back to the United States to take up residence in Fort Worth, Texas. Richard F. Celcer, a Texas scholar and author of *Hell's Half Acre*, writes that he was never able to establish that Place came to Fort Worth. On the other hand, Leonard Sanders, in his historical novel *Fort Worth*, quotes Delbert Willis of the *Fort Worth Press*, who argues that after Place left Sundance, she did, indeed, move to Fort Worth, where she opened up a brothel. But, when we consider the careful scholarship of Celcer, who spent ten years writing his book, it seems unlikely that Place was in that famous cow town. There are other arguments, too. Richard Llewellyn, author of *How Green Was My Valley*, suggests that Place got tired of the outlaw way of life and married an important government official in Paraguay. Yet, most scholars can find no documentation to back up Llewellyn's claim.

What we do know is this: In 1903, Pinkerton Detective Frank Dimaio went to South America to apprehend the two famous outlaws and their female sidekick and bring them to justice. The Pinkerton Detective Agency had spent a great deal of money trying to track down Butch Cassidy and the Sundance Kid—to no avail. They collected every scrap of information they could find, and they came close to snagging the trio, but the bandits were always one step ahead.

As to the basic questions—where was she born, when did she die, what was her real name, what was her profession?—it's not clear we'll ever find those answers. Most outlaws and molls went by a *nom de guerre* to hide their identities and protect their families' reputations. Male outlaws were also protective of the women they associated with, and it wasn't just out of concern for the fairer sex. It was a way they protected themselves, too. If a lawman knew there was a sweetheart, a wife, or a favorite prostitute in a criminal's life, all he had to do was find her—and wait for the guy to show up. Butch Cassidy, perhaps the finest outlaw mind of the nineteenth century, knew this. He and the Wild Bunch vacationed in the better bawdy houses in Texas, but practiced their profession a thousand miles away (usually in the Rocky Mountain West). If there was a girl they fancied, and there were a number of them, the gang tried to keep her identity masked so she couldn't be used as bait. It was only when Sundance and Place were sure that they would leave the United States for good that they indulged in a sentimental photo.

Thanks to this lapse in judgment, lawmen finally learned what Place looked like.

In the meantime, historians will keep chasing after Etta Place. She's still one of the most wanted women in the land. ⇥

CHAPTER THIRTEEN

LITTLE BRITCHES AND CATTLE ANNIE

Teenybopper Bad Girls

In the mid-1890s, William M. Doolin was a very wanted man. His wayward career was an inspiration for two young girls—Jennie Stevens, aka "Little Britches," and Anna McDoulet, aka "Cattle Annie"—who would soon be two of the most famous female outlaws in the last days of the Old West.

If you met Bill Doolin on the street, he might be the sort of fellow who would ruffle your kid's hair, compliment your wife on her new hat, or buy you a drink. You'd never know he was the head of the Doolin Gang and an alumnus of the infamous Dalton Gang. William Doolin was also a friend of Cole Younger and Jessie James. Like Butch Cassidy, he was personable and intelligent and able to attract some of the best outlaw talent for his gang.

Also like Butch Cassidy, he recognized that he couldn't survive without the help of the common folks, and so he did his best to curry their favor. He was generous with drinks and free with his money, and he won the hearts of the common folk by robbing their common enemies: the banks, the trains, and the express offices. For nearly five years, townspeople and ranchers from the Panhandle to Missouri were tight-lipped about his whereabouts when the law came looking for him.

Jennie Stevens and Anna McDoulet, soon to be known as "Little Britches" and "Cattle Annie," were among the girls who were taken with the infamous charmer. Both Oklahoma girls had helped with chores and worked from dawn to dusk their entire lives—with nothing to show for it. Their families hired them out as domestics to bring much-needed money into the family coffers. Doolin and his gang of thieves were the closest thing this pair of teenagers had to heroes. They appeared to have everything the two girls had never enjoyed: fame, prestige, wealth, and leisure.

They'd see Doolin in the area and admired the good life he lived. He hardly worked—unless he was unholstering his Colts to rob some rich people now and again. It didn't take long before the ambitious pair decided to follow in his footsteps. Stevens and McDoulet decided they were done with sore backs, dirty fingernails, and faded dresses. They wanted to live like Doolin.

They succeeded, too. For a brief time, the girls would be celebrities, known nationwide as the eyes and lookouts for the Doolin Gang. Surprisingly, they lived to tell about it.

Jennie Stevens was born in 1879 in Barton County, Missouri, to Daniel and Lucy Stevens. The family eked out a living; everyone worked hard just to put enough food on the table. When Jennie was eight years old, the Stevens family moved nearer to Indian country, close to the Missouri border. Later the family uprooted again and moved to Pawnee County, Oklahoma. Young Jennie would daydream about what life would be like if she had money—or if she were an outlaw. Bandit sightings and stories were fairly common in that country. The James Gang, the Younger Gang, the Dalton Gang, the Doolin Gang, and Belle Starr were all topics of conversation.

Stevens acquired all the skills a typical frontier boy would learn. She understood cattle and horses and was reputed to be a crack shot. (Of course, it should be noted that nearly every woman we've discussed in this book was reported by the media or in folklore to be a crack shot.) When she was fifteen, she'd had enough of dirt farming. She dressed up in men's clothes and ran away from home. The pants were way too big and hung off her small frame. Ironically, she became known as "Little Britches."

Stevens' first foray into the criminal world wasn't promising. She tried to join a gang of bad guys. The "goodhearted" outlaws dumped her off at a neighbor's house with instructions to return her to her father. To add insult to injury, on her first adventure into crime, she lost one of her family's horses (a horse the poor Stevens family could ill afford to lose). Angered and embarrassed that his daughter would do such a foolish thing, her father gave her a sound whipping.

Stevens decided there was only one thing she could do: run off and marry. At age sixteen she wed horse trader Benjamin Midkiff, in Newkirk, Oklahoma, in 1895. Midkiff was not exactly the man of her dreams, but he offered the potential for life outside the farm.

The couple lived in Perry, Oklahoma, where Stevens was not the perfect wife. While Midkiff was gone on business, she was caught in some compromising situations with other men. When he found out, Midkiff unceremoniously dumped her off at her father's and left her for good. The marriage had only lasted six months. The same year, Stevens was said to have married a man named Robert Stephens. That relationship didn't last long, either. Stevens was sixteen, twice married, and still looking to better her life.

Her soon-to-be partner, Anna McDoulet, was born in Lawrence, Kansas, in 1879, to James and Rebekah McDoulet. The McDoulet family, too, was impoverished. No one is quite certain what her father did for work. But when Anna was about four, the family moved to Coyville, Kansas. To bring in cash, the young girl was hired out to do household chores and possibly work in a hotel. When Anna was twelve, the McDoulets moved to the Cherokee Nation, and it appears she studied at a mission school and worked in a restaurant in the evening. When she was fourteen, the family moved yet again to another reservation not far from Tulsa, Oklahoma, in a place called Skiatook. It was there that the young McDoulet started to show an affinity for outlaws. Like Jennie Stevens, she longed for the glamour and the good life associated with crime.

The two sixteen-year-olds met at a community dance—cowboys would ride fifty miles for a chance to dance with a pretty girl—and became instant best friends, discovering they had a lot in common.

At another dance, much to her delight, McDoulet met a good-looking man. When McDoulet found out he was the infamous "Red Buck" George Waightman, a member of the Doolin Gang, she instantly fell in love. Red Buck, named for his mop of red hair, was from Texas and had a charming side, but he also had a mean streak that made him willing to shoot a man—face-to-face or in the back. He was also worth about $5,000 in reward money, dead or alive. While Red had swept McDoulet off her feet, the romantic interest was one sided. As far as he was concerned, she was just another teenage farm girl with a crush.

Despite the rejection, the two wannabe bandits got to know the other members of the gang. The outlaws didn't take their aspirations as seriously as the girls had hoped, but they didn't entirely discount them either. The gang, not surprisingly, did let the girls wash and mend their clothing and do some cooking. But this wasn't enough for Stevens and McDoulet.

The two young women seemed to figure if they dressed the part, perhaps they'd be accepted. They put away their dresses and slipped into the outlaw duds they so admired: shirts, pants, neckerchiefs, and boots. In the mid-1890s, this was a radical step indeed. And then they took it a shocking step further: Instead of riding sidesaddle, they rode their horses like men, strapped on Colts with cartridge belts, and carried rifles. From a distance, at least, they actually looked like men. They gradually earned the trust of the outlaws and were allowed to perform additional tasks. Besides the more domestic skills—cooking, mending, and washing—the two girls carried messages between members of the gang, served as lookouts, and were the eyes and ears of the wanted men. It was their job to see if any lawmen were planning a raid. However, while they were working with the gang, they were never considered more than useful tagalongs. They were not accepted as full-fledged outlaws—which was frustrating for both of the teens.

If the gang wouldn't accept them as legitimate members, they'd prove their outlaw worth by going out on their own. There was a learning curve to being a world-class bank and train robber. You had to start on the simpler crimes first and work your way up. So, to catch the gang's attention and prove their worth, the girls focused on crimes they could

Teenagers Cattle Annie (Anna McDoulet) and Little Britches (Jennie Stevens)
admired the Dalton and Doolin gangs and were determined to be outlaws.

handle. Because they'd both grown up around horses and cattle, they decided to officially become stock rustlers.

When rustling failed to secure them positions in the gang, the two girls branched out into the thriving and lucrative bootleg liquor trade—selling illegal whiskey to the Pawnee and Osage Indians. While selling whiskey was illegal, it wasn't as risky as rustling cattle: a bootlegger would only get ten to forty days in the local jail, while a rustler could get strung up from the nearest cottonwood tree or do some serious jail time.

By 1895, Stevens and McDoulet were making news—much to their delight. "Cattle Annie" became McDoulet's media sobriquet for obvious reasons. "Little Britches" had already been Stevens' outlaw nickname. Newspaper stories about Cattle Annie and Little Britches, the teenage rustler/outlaws with the Doolin Gang, were very popular with readers. Tall tales grew about the two lady "bad guys." They were never more than nickel-and-dime rustlers and bootleggers, but the press had them committing major robberies—some hundreds of miles apart on the same day.

The girls were still in touch with the Doolin Gang—enjoying their new status, even if they still were not accepted as equals. They were not above assuming disguises—putting on dresses and fixing their hair and going into town and working in a restaurant or hotel, keeping their ears open for any information that the gang could use about impending raids or other helpful tidbits. They proved to be valuable assets. At one point, when a group of lawmen was closing in on the gang, the sheriffs ran into the teens on a road and questioned them. The girls were able to warn the gang—some say by a shot, others say it was a written message—and the gang slipped away.

After a while, their antics no longer seemed cute. They'd become a nuisance, if not an embarrassment, for local officials. By late summer of 1895, Stevens was arrested for rustling and selling whiskey. She managed to get away, however, when her guard took her to a restaurant for dinner. It appears he spent too much time looking at her pretty face. She sweet-talked him, and when he wasn't looking, she zipped out the backdoor and rode off on the nearest horse.

Stevens met up with McDoulet, and the duo tried to flee, but they had not counted on the determination and skill of deputy U.S. Marshal

Sheriff Bill Tilghman. By the next evening, Tilghman had reportedly found the teen bandits holed up in a shack. Shots were exchanged. Cattle Annie was caught escaping out a window and taken into custody. Little Britches managed to escape on a horse. Tilghman is said to have chased after the fleeing teen. Stevens is reported to have fired a few shots over her shoulder at the sheriff. The veritable lawman, not wanting to shoot a woman, is said to have blasted her horse out from under her while they were both at a full gallop. Both Cattle Annie and Little Britches were taken to jail, making them nationally recognized celebrities.

In September of 1895, the two sixteen-year-olds were brought before the Fourth Judicial District of Oklahoma Territory. They were tried for selling whiskey to the Indians and for cattle rustling. Judge Andrew G. Curtain passed sentence upon them, giving them each a year in prison at Framingham, Massachusetts. They were finally the outlaws they wanted to be. They boarded the train to Framingham with fanfare; the public was eager to see these young celebrity criminals. They looked upon their trip as an adventure into a brave new world. For two young ladies who had never been more than a few miles from home, this must have seemed like a voyage of discovery.

Once they were behind bars, however, their fame disappeared. The public wanted to read about the latest bandits and holdups. As Little Britches and Cattle Annie, they were front-page fodder, but as Jennie Stevens and Annie McDoulet, they were just two prison inmates.

The teens were paroled for good behavior; newspaper accounts vary on the year. Stevens headed back to Oklahoma, married, had a family, and lived the rest of her life on the straight and narrow. McDoulet stayed back East and was employed as a domestic helper until she died of consumption within a year of her release from prison. ⤙

SKIRTS, FLIRTS, AND SIX-GUNS

EXCEPTIONAL VERVE AND VICIOUSNESS

SOME WOMEN IN THE WEST WEREN'T MERELY accessories or petty thieves; they were the masterminds behind serious crimes and committed unthinkably violent deeds. A woman carrying out this level of crime was a rare and noteworthy thing indeed.

Cora Hubbard was the driving force behind an 1897 Missouri bank robbery. Madam Vestal facilitated the infamous Deadwood Stage robberies and is said to have blasted an ex-lover who cheated her. Pearl Hart is one of a small handful of women who actually robbed a stage. She held up the coach with her lover, six-gun in hand, and personally took the money off each passenger. She botched the getaway, but she was proud of her part in the caper.

Crimes of passion were a little more understandable. In a heat of rage, infamous gambler Madam Moustache is said to have pulled the trigger and fatally shot a man who had cheated her out of everything she had.

Ah Toy, meanwhile, was one of the most corrupt women in the history of the Old West. A madam and brothel owner in San Francisco, she trafficked in the flesh trade, importing scores of young Chinese girls who were sold into slavery as prostitutes.

The women in this chapter definitely earned the distinction of outlaw.

CHAPTER FOURTEEN

CORA HUBBARD

Bank Robbing Belle

━━◆━━

Had she been a man, Cora Hubbard would have been just one more second-rate outlaw who aspired to make it in the world of crime— someone who fought the system and lost. What sets Hubbard apart is that she was perhaps the first member of an exclusive club. Hubbard was one of very few women in the Old West to have robbed a bank. And she was credited as the heist's mastermind.

The southwestern Missouri woods were hot and humid when the trio of outlaws made camp outside of town in August 1897. Cora Hubbard, then twenty-seven, was the leader of the so-called Hubbard Gang, which included Whit Tennyson, a drifter, and John Sheets, a day laborer who had an outlaw past and claimed to be an experienced bank robber. On August 17, the three bandits were set to ride into the quiet town of Pineville, Missouri, and rob the McDonald County Bank. They imagined the money they would take would be the stuff of dreams. Cora Hubbard's job was to watch the men's backs and hold the horses for their getaway. In an interview later in her life, she says she felt a surge of excitement and was not afraid.

Hubbard was born in 1870 and lost her mother at an early age. She grew up watching her father, Sam Hubbard, break his back in the coal mines near Weir City, Kansas, eking out a living. Hubbard wanted no part of that kind of life, and she didn't want to grow old as a poor farmer's wife, either. She wanted the good things in life—but didn't want to work for them.

Hubbard married but realized her prospects for bettering herself were dwindling. She divorced her first husband in the spring of 1897. By July 1, 1897, she had married Bud Parker and moved to a farm outside of Nowata, Oklahoma. Parker had greater expectations for himself and his future. He might be the man who could make her happy and not disappoint her. It was at this time an idea was starting to take fruition—an idea she had pondered for some time. Maybe her ticket to the good life was on the outlaw trail. All one needed was a Colt six-gun, a Winchester rifle, a fast horse, and courage.

Hubbard had no lack of local role models where criminal life was concerned. Outlaws were her heroes. The infamous Dalton Gang had achieved a cult status among the common folks in Kansas and Oklahoma. Cora Hubbard was no exception. She had studied Bob Dalton's life and idolized him. He was a common man who had refused to be poor; he robbed from the rich and lived the good life. She admired that. She also identified with Belle Starr, reading everything she could about her. Starr was a woman and thus a special source of inspiration. After Hubbard was arrested for her own crimes, she was especially pleased that the papers sometimes referred to her as "the second Belle Starr." She also followed the accounts of Cattle Annie and Little Britches. If these women could carve a name for themselves in the world of crime, so could she.

Hubbard met up with John Sheets when he began working as a laborer on her husband's farm. Whit Tennyson was a drifter who likely worked for the couple in exchange for meals. He was a big talker and a braggart who boasted about robbing banks and riding the outlaw trail.

With Cora Hubbard's aspiration for the outlaw life and Tennyson's bragging, the next step was easy. With Tennyson's help, and encouraged by John Sheets, she spearheaded what she thought were foolproof robbery plans. Her husband, Parker, agreed to help. So did Hubbard's two brothers, Bill and Al Hubbard. Bill had once lived in Pineville and was the one who suggested the bank. He had drawn up rough plans and agreed to go into the bank with Tennyson.

In preparation for her outlaw debut, Hubbard, meanwhile, sported a new look: she cut her hair like a man's and wore pants. Before the bank heist, however, she had a rude awakening; her new husband and her brothers weren't quite as ready as she was to become lawbreakers. The actual prospect of saddling up the horses and buckling on guns sobered them up. By the time they were ready to leave, some of the Hubbard Gang started to get cold feet. It was one thing to plan and talk about a robbery; it was something else entirely to strap on weapons and ride into a town and steal money at gunpoint. Hubbard was upset with her brothers, but felt immensely betrayed by her husband. She later told a reporter that she would not "stay married to a damned coward."

Hubbard went on to rob the bank with Tennyson and Sheets. On the morning of August 17, the two men slipped into Pineville to case the bank while Hubbard waited in camp. The coast looked clear. Her two partners rode back and picked her up. Not far from the bank, Cora held the horses while the two men headed in. (She might be the ringleader, but the men still wielded the Colts and did the serious dirty work.) It was a slow day at the bank; banking officials and the teller were on the front porch chatting. Sheets forced them back inside the bank while Tennyson stayed at the door in case someone approached. Sheets demanded money, and the frightened bank clerks filled a bag with cash and handed it over. Instead of tying the bankers up and leaving them in the bank, however, Sheets and Tennyson marched the men at gunpoint down the street to where Hubbard had the horses. This was a bold move, if not a bit stupid; if they'd tied them up and left them in the bank, they might have been able to slip away without drawing attention to themselves.

The two men reached Hubbard, they set the relieved clerks free, and the trio raced out of town with the $590 they had stolen. In no time, an angry posse was thrown together, and the townsmen were hot on their trail. It didn't take long for the lawmen to figure out that the bandits were going to reverse their course and head for Indian country; the inexperienced outlaws were more predictable than they'd realized. The posse set up a trap. Sure enough, the Hubbard Gang rode into it.

Six men with Winchester long guns and shotguns waited to ambush the robbers. Firing a bit too soon, when they were still slightly out of range, the posse merely winged Tennyson and Sheets with a shotgun blast. Hubbard emptied her pistol at the posse. One of the deputies sustained a minor wound. Tennyson got separated from Hubbard and Sheets in the deep woods.

Lawmen caught Tennyson on August 19. His wounds were cared for and he was thrown in jail. Not being half as bad or tough as he'd boasted, Tennyson ratted out his desperate partners, giving the law everything except their shoe sizes. Officials had the leads they needed to effectively trail the other two.

Sheets' horse had been shot and killed in the shootout, so he and Hubbard shared a horse. Near the Kansas border, Hubbard robbed a man of his horse so Sheets would have a mount. In Kansas, they split up.

On August 21, Hubbard bought a train ticket for Weir City, her father's home. Sheets had taken another route and agreed to meet her there in several days. Hubbard had too much pride to return to her husband—besides, she thought him a coward.

Because of Tennyson's statement, deputies knew where to find her. She had just arrived at her father's home; she had discarded her men's clothing and was in a dress when there was a rap on the door. Hubbard found herself facing the barrel of a rifle. She put her hands over her head and was taken, barefoot, to jail. (Her brothers and father were also jailed but were soon released when it was discovered they hadn't participated in the robbery.) While she was imprisoned, she agreed to dress up in men's clothing similar to what she wore during the robbery and hold an empty rifle so a photographer could take her picture.

By August 24, officials still hadn't found any of the stolen money—until someone decided to look in the garden. In jars near some pepper and potato plants, they found $166. Two days later, Sheets showed up at the Hubbard home and was quickly taken without incident and jailed. He had nearly $100 from the bank job and several firearms. In ten days,

Cora Hubbard poses in men's clothing and holds a gun. A photographer came to the prison and asked if he could photograph the famous bandit in clothing similar to what she wore when she and the Hubbard Gang robbed the McDonald County Bank in Pineville, Missouri. She is believed to be the only woman in the Old West to rob a bank. MCDONALD COUNTY LIBRARY, PINEVILLE, MISSOURI.

the Hubbard Gang had been captured and most of the stolen money had been returned to the McDonald County Bank.

By the end of August, the three outlaws were headed to trial. By January of the next year, each had been convicted of their crime. Whit Tennyson got ten years. John Sheets and Cora Hubbard got twelve years. (Apparently Tennyson's sentence was cut because he squealed.) Hubbard served seven years in a Missouri state prison and was released for good behavior. After prison, she drifted into obscurity. ⇒

Cora Hubbard, Whit Tennyson, and John Sheets, members of the Hubbard Gang, pose for a photo during their incarceration for bank robbery. Note that Tennyson and Sheets are handcuffed together. MCDONALD COUNTY LIBRARY, PINEVILLE, MISSOURI.

CHAPTER FIFTEEN

MADAM MOUSTACHE

A Double Shotgun Blast
FOR THE Lover Who Took All

During the 1850s and 1860s, Eleanora Dumont was one of the most successful gamblers on the frontier. Her first love was *vingt-et-un,*—a game known today as "twenty-one,"—but she was adept at any game of chance. This skillful gambler, who would one day come to be known as Madam Moustache, ran a number of successful gambling houses. In her parlors, she had the finest furnishings and the best liquor money could buy. She loved fine clothes and spent a small fortune on her attire.

Dumont also worked as a prostitute and a madam. A polite woman, she insisted that men not swear or use coarse language around her. She was known to gently correct them if they did. Despite her decorum, she was suspected of several murders, although nothing was proven in court.

Her history is shrouded. It is believed she was born in 1829, but historians don't know where. What is known is that the gambler who called herself Eleanora Dumont came to San Francisco in 1850 under the name Simone Jules. During the Gold Rush days, San Francisco was a town starved for women.

Prostitution was a booming business, but gambling brought in the big

Madam Moustache worked as a card dealer at the Bella Union, one of the great gambling houses in San Francisco during the Gold Rush. A miner with money to burn could gamble, see a show with women in racy costumes, enjoy an assortment of liquors at the bar, or purchase time with a prostitute. FROM J. H. BEADLE'S *THE UNDEVELOPED WEST*, UNIVERSITY OF MICHIGAN, MAKING OF AMERICA.

money. She went to work almost immediately at the Bella Union, one of the great gambling houses in San Francisco. She was hired as a card dealer, but she was probably expected to "entertain," too. She attracted an impressive clientele and made a great deal of money. In the Bella Union or its rival, the Parker House, a dealer might pay as much as $10,000 to $20,000 a month to rent a table in a good location. A private room could go for as high as $60,000 a month. Dumont liked high-stakes games and rented the best tables. Hundreds of thousands of dollars a day were wagered by miners who had money to burn and steam to blow off.

Dumont made a small fortune at the tables but was getting restless. By 1854, at age twenty-five, she had saved enough money to open her own gambling hall, Dumont House, in Nevada City, California—gold country.

She spared no expense on the Dumont House. She shipped in the finest furniture and fixtures money could buy. She stocked the bar with a wide selection of exotic wines and liqueurs. Her staff was friendly and

A typical scene in a western bar and gambling parlor; this one is in Leadville, Colorado. A female card dealer like Madam Moustache would have been a rarity and a big draw—sure to pack the house.
DENVER PUBLIC LIBRARY, WESTERN HISTORY COLLECTION, X-6363.

conciliatory, trained to pamper any man who had the money to pay his tab. Her establishment was considered an oasis in a rough and crude world. When she first opened her doors, drinks were on the house. Men lined up to toast the new proprietor with excellent champagne.

Dumont never ran crooked tables and was known for being fair. She loved to gamble and was very successful; playing cards came natural for her. It seemed she could look into the eye of a gambler and read him like a book.

However, when it came to the affairs of the heart, Dumont was not as successful. Men paid a great deal of attention to her; marriage proposals from successful businessmen were a weekly, if not daily, occurrence. In Nevada City, she fell in love with a man named Waite, a writer and an editor for the *Nevada Journal*. She did everything to get him to return her love, to no avail. She was prepared to give up the "sporting life" if he'd marry her, but Waite wasn't interested. He enjoyed Dumont's company and spent late evenings with her, but she wasn't the sort of woman he wanted to marry.

Depressed by her unrequited love, Dumont began drinking, something a careful gambler avoided. Soon the quick-witted gambler was off her game; her guard was down. She never saw the two-timing four-flusher coming to steal her heart—and her money. A slick named Lucky Dave came into her place and managed to talk her into taking him on as her junior partner. He took over much of the day-to-day operation of her house, and for a while things ran smoothly. He was paid a good wage, but he soon demanded a full partnership. He then became physically abusive and possessive; he wanted more control of her business. Lucky Dave also had begun stealing from the house and lining his pockets. By 1856, Dumont came to her senses and fired him.

Restless, she sold her business and headed for Virginia City, Nevada, and the Comstock Load. Dumont made a good living there, but still wasn't quite over Waite. She moved on to other boomtowns in the area. She tried her luck in Columbia, California. Impatient, she headed to Bannack, Montana, in 1864, opening up an elegant establishment. It was here that she picked up her famous nickname. A sore loser had noticed the hair on Eleanora Dumont's upper lip, which had gotten thicker of late. As he left the table, his poke empty, he spitefully lashed out, calling her "Madam Moustache." The moniker caught on.

After twenty years of working the boomtowns, Madam Moustache was ready to settle down. She wanted a quiet home away from the roulette wheels, the shuffle of cards, and the smell of whiskey. Like an old gunfighter, she had nothing left to prove and was ready to put down that deck of playing cards.

There had been many men in Madam Moustache's life, but no one she wanted to put her brand on—until she met a cattleman named Jack McNight. They married and bought a cattle ranch outside of Carson, Nevada. She had a beautiful ranch, money in the bank, and the man she loved. What could go wrong?

It didn't take long before her perfect world came crashing down like a poorly constructed house of cards. One morning she woke up and

Madam Moustache earned her nickname when hair started to grow on her upper lip. She made a fortune at the gambling tables and is believed to have shot and killed the man who stole her money and left her bankrupt.

An artist's rendition of Madam Moustache shooting the man who cheated her out of her ranch and savings. DENVER PUBLIC LIBRARY, WESTERN HISTORY COLLECTION, F-11608.

McNight was gone. She discovered the man of her dreams was the stuff of nightmares. In addition to stealing her heart, he took her jewelry, her money, and cleaned out her bank account.

She had no choice but to go back to the gaming halls, brothels, and bars. Devastated, she drank more heavily than ever. However, she had made one sacred promise to herself. She would personally kill the man who had ripped away her savings, her dignity, and her hope for a peaceful retirement in the high desert. She was not a stranger to weapons and knew how to pull back a hammer and squeeze the trigger.

While it couldn't be proven, and she denied it at the time, most folks in the area were pretty sure that Madam Moustache tracked down McNight and shot and killed him with her trusty 12-gauge. Some felt she had good reason to pull back the double hammers and that McNight got what he deserved. Little was done to investigate McNight's death.

Madam Moustache headed back to San Francisco and her old life at the gambling tables. She stayed until 1869 and gambled with some success, but she realized that she was not winning as many pots as she used to. So she set her sights on the mining camps of Montana. She also visited Deadwood, Dakota Territory; Cheyenne, Wyoming Territory; and Coeur d'Alene, Idaho Territory. In Colorado City, Colorado, she reportedly bullwhipped a man who tried to cheat her. She ran a gambling parlor/brothel in Tombstone, Arizona Territory, when Doc Holiday and Wyatt Earp, arguably the most famous and deadliest gunmen in the West, ruled the town. She'd have her girls dress up and ride about town in a carriage to drum up business. Despite her best efforts, Madam Moustache never made the kind of money she did earlier in her career.

In 1879, disillusioned, travel weary, dulled by the affects of alcohol, the fifty-year-old Dumont was desperate to change her luck. She headed east to Bodie, California, a boomtown high in the mountains. She played twenty-one, her game, in the Grand Central Saloon. But she kept drawing bad cards. She had lost her edge, as well as her gambling stake. Before she played through the deck, she lost everything and was completely broke again. Someone offered her a bottle. Numbed by her streak of bad luck, she took it and drank alone at the back of the saloon.

The next morning, Madam Moustache was dead. Her body was found at 8:00 A.M.; she was believed to have consumed poison. Several days after her death, the *Sacramento Union* reported that "a woman named Eleanora Dumont was found dead today one mile out of town, having committed suicide. She was well known in all the mining camps. Let her many good qualities evoke leniency in criticizing her failings."

The *Black Hills Daily Times*, in Deadwood, Dakota Territory, her old stomping grounds, stated:

> *A letter was received in this city, yesterday announcing the suicide of Madam Moustache, at Bodie, Cal. It seems that she . . . had run out of luck there [and] went broke and rather than be a strapped faro dealer on [this] mundane shore she took chances in that great undiscovered country from where no traveler ever returns. The Madam is well known in Deadwood, having run a game here during the years 1877-78.*

Out of respect for her, the folks of Bodie, California, took up a collection so she could be buried properly. Even though she was a gambler and a prostitute—a "fallen woman"—they buried her in the concentrated part of the cemetery. ⇥

CHAPTER SIXTEEN

PEARL HART

Arizona's Lady Stagecoach Robber

A true lady outlaw, even if she wasn't a very good one, was always a source of interest to the reading public—and to the sheriff who brought her in. When Sheriff Bill Truman of Pima County, Arizona, arrested Pearl Hart in 1899, he described her to the *Arizona Daily Star* as:

> *a tiger cat for verve and endurance. She looks feminine enough now, in the women's clothes I got for her, . . . and one can see the touch of a tasteful woman's hand in the way she has brightened up her cell. Yet, only a couple of days ago, I had a struggle with her for my life. She would have killed me in my tracks could she have gotten to her pistol. Sure women are curious creatures.*

Curious, indeed. Pearl Hart's wild foray into the crime world was apparently sparked out of a desire to help her mother. Hart's mother and sister had taken over the rearing of Hart's two children in Ontario, Canada. Around 1899, Hart received word from her older sister that their mother was very ill, and the medical bills were piling up.

Hart wasn't exactly in a position to offer financial assistance. Divorced from Frederick Hart, her first husband and father of her children, Pearl Hart was living with an aspiring miner named Joe Boot. His mining claims didn't pan out, so the couple turned to robbery. Hart would pretend to be a prostitute and try to lure drunken men to her room. When the amorous victim arrived, Boot would clobber him on the head and knock him senseless, at which point the pair would steal his money.

This worked for a while, until they were spotted and nearly arrested, managing to escape a few steps ahead of the law. After that scare, Hart came up with what she thought was a less risky plan. This scheme involved holding up the Benson-Globe Stage between Globe and Florence, Arizona.

Like so many of her outlaw sisters, Hart disguised herself as a man to carry out the crime. She cut her hair and donned a common miner's shirt and coveralls. With resolve, she tucked her pants into her boots and pulled on a cowboy hat. And on May 30, 1899, Hart and Boot stepped out in front of the stagecoach with their guns drawn. Boot held up the driver while Hart lightened the load of all three passengers. She got about $450 for her efforts; she reportedly gave each of her three victims some cash back so they'd have money for food and a hotel room. Then the desperados fired a few shots in the air and fled. They tried to put as much distance as they could between themselves and the posse that was sure to follow.

The trouble was, they got completely, hopelessly lost; Boot was about as good an outdoorsman as he was a miner. For two days, they wandered in circles—hungry, tired, and confused. On the third day, completely exhausted, they had to sleep. They woke up to Winchester and Colt bores in their faces, thanks to a posse led by Sheriff Bill Truman. The pair had made it only a few miles from the hold-up site.

At first Hart seemed compliant; she told Truman her name and the name of her partner in crime. (Joe Boot was probably not his real name, but it's the only name historians have for him.) Then Hart tried to bolt, forcing Truman to wrestle her to the ground. As the sheriff commented later, "She was anxious not to get to jail." The *Arizona Daily Star* characterized Hart as "a wild-cat woman and had she not been relieved of her [weapon] a bloody foray might have resulted."

Bank-robber Pearl Hart poses for a photographer in 1899 while in prison awaiting trial. The lawmen were careful to unload the firearms before allowing her to hold them for the photo. ARIZONA HISTORICAL SOCIETY, TUCSON.

The two bandits were charged and held in the Florence, Arizona, jail. Hart was later moved to the jail in Tucson because it had better facilities for women. The media had a field day with her arrest and trial, and she seemed to enjoy the notoriety, eagerly giving interviews and signing autographs. Crowds of people would sometimes gather around the jail to get a glimpse of the pretty lady who robbed a stage. National newspapers and magazines, such as *Cosmopolitan*, arrived in droves to interview her in jail. Enjoying his time in the spotlight, Sheriff Truman fed the frenzy, telling the *Arizona Daily Star*, "She is a delicate dark haired woman, with little about her that would suggest the ability to hold up a stage loaded with frontiersmen. She had refined features, a mouth of the true rosebud type, and clear blue eyes that would be confounding to a baby." Hart soon became one of the most famous women in Arizona.

Newspapers credited Hart with being the first and only female stagecoach bandit in the West. However, a woman named Jane Kirkham had beaten her to this dubious honor in 1879, when she robbed a stage near Buena Vista, Colorado. Kirkham was killed in the robbery and never had time to become a national sensation.

What led Hart down her dusty road to fame? She was born Pearl Lindsay in approximately 1872 in Lindsay, Ontario, Canada. She attended boarding school and received a better-than-average education for a girl in her day. Her mother hoped boarding school would quell Pearl's adventurous spirit. It didn't. And Pearl wasn't above running away from school when she got bored with the routine.

During one of her adventures, Pearl met a rogue named Frederick Hart (some accounts refer to him as John Hart), a good-looking man who swept her off her feet. She was in love, but her family would have none of it. Pearl and Frederick Hart eloped. She was seventeen years old.

Frederick Hart dreamed of being a full-time gambler. Unfortunately, he wasn't very good at it and always seemed to spend more money than he made. Worse, he was also reputed to be a heavy drinker who abused Pearl physically. Pearl frequently left him but would come back when he promised to straighten up his life. Eventually, the cycle would start again: He would lose money, fall into hopeless debt and poverty, then start beating Pearl. The couple lived from hand to mouth. Hart went

In prison, Pearl Hart was not only photographed in her outlaw garb, but she was also asked to dress in more traditional women's attire for photographers.
ARIZONA HISTORICAL SOCIETY, TUCSON.

from job to job, gambling all the while. They had two children during these turbulent years. Wanting more for them than she could give, she tearfully left her kids with her mother and her sister—and she stayed with Frederick Hart.

She later told reporters that during her lowest times she turned to prostitution; some sources say she also used drugs such as marijuana and morphine. She admitted in an interview that her husband prostituted her for rent money on several occasions. She claimed she enjoyed the world's oldest trade and liked "the sociability, conversation, and good times."

The couple moved to Chicago in 1893 so Frederick could work as a barker at one of the exhibits at the World's Columbian Exposition. Pearl worked odd jobs, but she also had plenty of free time to wander about the Exposition, listening to lectures and seeing shows. The Exposition experience changed her life.

The wild west shows got Pearl's attention, and sharpshooter Annie Oakley, sometimes known as "Little Miss Sure Shot," particularly intrigued her. Pearl soon developed a fascination with firearms and shooting. What was more, she wanted to see and experience the West and had a great desire to travel to the frontier and see the vast plains and rugged mountains.

Pearl was also intrigued by the ideas discussed at the Women's Pavilion by the famous feminist Julian Ward Howe, among other suffragettes of the day.

Pearl was determined to move west, specifically to Trinidad, Colorado. And so she did—without Frederick. The facts about her life in Trinidad are unclear. What is known is that she reconciled with Frederick one more time in the late 1890s and then finally gave up on the marriage for good; the couple divorced.

She met Joe Boot in 1899 in Arizona. In an interview later in her life, she said he was a wonderful man and she loved him. At other times, she said he was useless. According to the loquacious Sheriff Truman, she expressed "nothing but contempt for her companion."

Her true feelings will never be known, but the duo certainly managed to find trouble together. When Hart was still in the Tucson jail for the stagecoach robbery she and Boot pulled, she got a little stir crazy and decided to bust out and feel the fresh air again. She found a willing accomplice in Ed Hogan, a jail trustee who had been incarcerated for drunkenness. The two jailbirds decided to create a hole in the wall of her prison cell. On October 20, 1899, the *Tucson Star* reported, "After everything was quiet . . . it was the work of a few minutes to cut a hole through the wall into Pearl's room. She held a sheet to catch the plaster. After the hole was cut through, she put a sheet underneath, and placing her chair upon that crawled through the hole." Hart was recaptured a few days later in New Mexico and brought back to jail in Tucson.

In late 1899, the celebrity outlaw was tried for the stagecoach robbery. Hart put on quite a show for the court. Using the court as a platform to expound on her views of feminism, she flatly stated that no court of men had the authority to put her on trial. She argued, "I shall not consent to be tried under a law in which my sex had no voice in making."

After a heated trial, the jury acquitted Pearl Hart. Her partner in crime, Joe Boot, was sentenced to thirty years at the Yuma Territorial Prison. In 1901, he escaped from prison and fled to Mexico, never to be seen again.

Judge Fletcher Dolan was livid that the jury had acquitted Hart. He urged prosecutors to charge her with stealing a pistol from the driver of the stage. Hart was immediately charged, tried, and convicted of the crime and sentenced to five years at the Yuma Territorial Prison.

While serving her time, Hart continued to grant interviews, although some of the public interest in her had ebbed. She described her dream of a career as a performer, perhaps in a wild west show. She even talked to a playwright who wanted to write a play about her life and cast her as the star once she was out of prison.

Hart's stay in prison was short but eventful. She had special privileges and a private cell—a rarity for Yuma, which sometimes crammed ten inmates into one cell. But she wanted out. So Hart told the authorities that she was pregnant. She might have been. It wouldn't have been above her to get pregnant—or to simply say she was. The problem was the only two male visitors she'd had were the governor and a local minister. Not wanting to cause a scandal, the prison board felt it was in everyone's best interest to grant her parole.

On December 19, 1902, Hart walked out the door a free woman. She soon discovered, to her dismay, that she had become old news. History lost track of her, and legend once again filled in the gaps. It is said she tried her hand at acting, resorted to prostitution, or even moved back to Ontario, where she lived quietly with her kids and aging mother.

It is believed Pearl Hart died in the 1950s, but the legend of this famous stagecoach robber lives on. ⊁

CHAPTER SEVENTEEN

MADAM VESTAL

The Faro Queen AND THE Deadwood Highway Woman

⊹⊱————⊰⊹

Awoman of exceptional beauty, Belle Siddons, later known as Madam Vestal, intuitively knew how to use every bit of grace and charm nature had given her. She was impeccably dressed and perfectly mannered. From a young age, she knew how to flatter men, making flirtation an art form.

Siddons was born in Cole County, Missouri, near Jefferson City, circa 1840, and grew up in an influential plantation-owning family in St. Louis, Missouri. A complete Southern gentlewoman, she attended the best schools, including a prestigious woman's university in Lexington, Kentucky.

When the Civil War broke out, Belle used her charisma to influence the young men of her acquaintance to fight for the Confederacy. However, for a romantic, patriotic, young Southern woman, this wasn't enough. She decided to employ her charms in a more worthwhile endeavor. Belle Siddons became a Confederate spy.

In 1862, Siddons cultivated friendships with the occupying Union forces, specifically the officers. She was a perfect hostess and escort. She knew that soldiers liked to talk in front of a pretty girl so they could impress her. Siddons slipped valuable information about Union troop movement and supply lines to Confederate officials. She would put the information on small slips of paper, which she would hide in her clothing or her effects, and deliver the notes to her network of Confederate contacts—a very dangerous practice, given the damaging information they contained. The beautiful young Confederate spy proved an asset to rebel troops in the assault on Union supply lines.

Soon Union leaders began to suspect her. Discretion would have been the better part of espionage, but not for this young spy. Instead of lying low until reservations abated, Siddons continued to gather information—and without much subtlety. She was convinced she was too clever to be caught in a Union trap. And in the unlikely event she was arrested, she was sure her status with the Union officers, her good looks, and social graces would protect her.

Late in 1862, General Samuel R. Curtis of the Union army ordered officers to bring Siddons in for questioning. Before she was picked up, she was tipped off by a Northern suitor. Instead of fleeing, she stuck around to gather a little more information—and was spotted and brought to General Curtis. Siddons hadn't had time to get rid of the incriminating information she carried, and it didn't look good. General Curtis informed her that the penalty for spying was firing squad or imprisonment; he locked her up until further notice. Sitting in a prison cell sobered her, but she never lost her poise or charm. Siddons was able to work out a deal with the general so she would not have to spend the duration of the war in prison. In the winter of 1863, she was part of a prisoner exchange, and she had to promise to work in a hospital and never fight against the North again. Siddons kept her word.

When the Civil War ended, Siddons returned to Fort Jefferson, Missouri, and worked to promote Southern interests during Reconstruction. She met a gentleman named Newt Hallet, fell in love, and married. The couple moved to Texas, where Hallet could expand his business. Tragically, a yellow fever epidemic took him before they had been married two years. Mourning the loss of her husband and angry over the outcome of the war, something snapped inside of Belle Siddons, and she was never the same again. Still outwardly charming, Siddons harbored a hidden bitterness that would never leave her.

Disillusioned, Siddons left behind her life of Southern gentility to work as a gambler in the West. Although aware she would be considered no better than a prostitute, she had learned that honor, especially dead Southern honor, wouldn't put food on her table or pay her rent. Now her fortune would rest with the toss of the dice or turn of the card. Lonely miners and cowboys would be willing to play with a pretty woman.

She studied games of chance from the dealer's point of view. Siddons was a fast learner and proved to be a shrewd gambler. And she played the men as adroitly and carefully as she played games of chance. She made a reputation for herself in Cheyenne, Fort Hayes, and Wichita. Her large gambling tent on Blake Street in Denver was quite successful.

Whether it was roulette, keno, poker, or blackjack, she played all with equal ease. Her favorite game, however, was faro, and soon she became known as the Faro Queen. Siddons had a talent for making each gambler feel important. She encouraged the players to stare into her eyes or at her ample bosom, making them forget they were losing—or at least not mind so much.

By the mid-1870s, Belle Siddons had changed her name to the mysterious Madam Vestal. Men lined up to gamble with this woman who had become a frontier legend. By 1876, she was tiring of Denver. Siddons was making a small fortune, but it was not enough. Her goal was to make it big, and her gambler's nose told her that Deadwood in Dakota Territory could be her gold mine.

After making the long journey from Colorado, Madam Vestal wasted no time opening up a gambling house. She drew eager men to her tables, men who had gold to spare. Millions of dollars in gold were being taken out of the gulch, and Madam Vestal did her share to lighten the loads of the prospering miners. Her business thrived, but she was still not satisfied.

Madam Vestal could pull gold out of miners' pockets, but there was a bigger prize: Tens of thousands of dollars in gold were being shipped out of Deadwood by stagecoach. She was determined to get her share of it. She had been successful getting Union men to talk during the Civil War; surely she could put those talents to use again. At her gambling tables,

Deadwood, Dakota Territory, during the Gold Rush.
NEBRASKA STATE HISTORICAL SOCIETY, #20080017.

miners, mining and transportation officials, and others openly discussed confidential gold shipments. It wouldn't take much subtle coaxing to learn more about where and when—and how much. Sometimes these men even had impromptu planning meetings over a game of cards, discussing the strategic particulars. The pretty lady was, after all, just a pretty lady, so what did it matter if they talked business in front of her.

Madam Vestal began to form discreet associations with some unsavory characters who frequented her parlor—men who were known outlaws. She paid particular interest to an intelligent highwayman named Archie Cummings, the leader of a band of outlaws. This road agent was bold and daring, and she liked his style. Cummings was an ex-Southerner guerilla fighter from Kansas, something she thought showed character. She knew by his look that he was interested in her. Before long, Cummings had fallen madly in love with the famous gambler.

At first, Madam Vestal passed information about gold shipments to Cummings. His gang would then rob the stages, and they would all split the loot. She enjoyed the lucrative kickbacks, but she wanted a more active role and a bigger cut of the riches. Soon she started to help plan the holdups with Cummings. They became quite successful— too successful.

Officials began to suspect that Madam Vestal was somehow involved in the robberies. On several occasions, her gambling parlor was raided, but nothing was found. Archie Cummings pleaded with her to stop the holdups. Madam Vestal should have left well enough alone or put her plans on hold. Surely she knew that once she became a suspect, every move she made would be watched. It seems greed clouded her logic.

To help combat the scourge of robberies, two new super coaches were brought in from Wyoming. The fortified stages were armored with metal plates and had a safe, which was bolted to the floor and sides of the coach. Known as "messengers," men armed with rifles and sawed-off shotguns locked themselves inside. One of the stages was called *Monitor*, the other *Ironsides*. These war wagons helped prevent robberies, but they didn't stop the holdups entirely.

To figure out who was responsible for the robberies, officials hired a tough guy named Daniel Boone May to go undercover. He was a bounty hunter and gunfighter. He was bold, tough, and cunning, and he had strayed over the legal line a time or two. Author Rolf Johnson's firsthand description of May in *Happy As a Sunflower: Adventures in the West, 1875–1880* paints a picture of a striking individual: "His eyes were a peculiar feature, being of an indescribable hue between yellow, green and grey, and had a curious restless look about them. He was a man I would instinctively fear without knowing who he was." His job was to stop the robberies by infiltrating the gangs who were holding up the Deadwood line. His cover was a stage driver. His specific target was Madam Vestal.

Born in Missouri in 1852, May was one of the few men who could get the better of the Faro Queen. She found that she was attracted to this big, raw-boned stranger and was flattered by his attention. Her infatuation for May caused her to lose her objectivity, although she still had enough sense not to ignite jealousy between her chief henchman, Cummings, and May. May played his own effective game with Madam Vestal, pretending to be an outlaw who wanted in on the action. It didn't

Deadwood law enforcement hired Daniel Boone May, a bounty hunter and gunfighter, to gain the confidence of Madam Vestal and find who was responsible for the gold heists. WYOMING STATE ARCHIVES, DEPARTMENT OF STATE PARKS AND CULTURAL RESOURCES, #2461.

take long before he had learned enough about her operation to take action and put a stop to it.

May would have to act quickly because Madam Vestal had already planned to leave Deadwood for San Francisco. May soon learned that the lovesick Cummings and his cronies had just smuggled her money out of town and planned to meet her in California.

May knew the outlaws were headed to Cheyenne to catch a train, and he tipped off Cheyenne police, who held Archie Cummings and his gang until May got there. May and a partner took custody of the outlaws and asked the men where the money was. The outlaws refused to answer. Acting on vigilante justice, May hung the highwaymen one by one until only Cummings was left.

Cummings agreed to take May to where he hid the strongbox en route from Deadwood to Cheyenne. Cummings assumed he could make a deal and perhaps walk away with part of the loot for his cooperation—or at least his freedom. When May retrieved the box of gold, Cummings thought he had it made, but he was wrong. May decided to hang Cummings anyway.

When Madam Vestal got word of what had happened, she was devastated. Her partner in love and crime was dead, May had made a fool of her, and her money was gone.

Although Madam Vestal never faced prosecution for her illegal activities, due to lack of evidence, the community knew she'd been involved in the robberies and wanted nothing to do with her. For the first time in her life she started to drink—a lot. Madam Vestal was so despondent that she attempted to kill herself with poison; her stomach was pumped and she survived.

The Faro Queen had fallen from gambling grace. Her association with the robbers made her *persona non grata* in Deadwood. She left before she was run out.

The crystal-eyed gambler, with sharp wits and a keen understanding of men, was now lost. In 1879, she opened up a gambling parlor and dancehall in Leadville, Colorado, but her enterprise proved fruitless. Men no longer lined up to play her games of chance. Where she had been a high roller, she now played two-bit ante. Madam Vestal was drinking more heavily by then and had stopped taking care of herself. She became a gambling vagabond, hitting all the boomtowns—trying to run third-rate gambling joints from Tombstone, Arizona, to Leadville, Colorado. Not satisfied with the bottle, she began smoking opium and quickly became an addict.

Madam Vestal finally managed to make it to California in 1880, ending up in San Francisco. Ill and defeated by opium and life, she died in a transient hospital in 1881, just four years after leaving Deadwood. ⊷

CHAPTER EIGHTEEN

AH TOY

An Exploited Woman

EXPLOITS

Others

In her native China, Ah Toy was a victim of an unforgiving social system in which girls and women were, at best, undervalued, second-class citizens. She was further confronted by the prejudices and brutal realities of the American West. Nevertheless, Ah Toy carved out a living on the San Francisco waterfront in the sex trade, running a successful, albeit corrupt, business in a world few women, especially Chinese women, dared to enter. Unlike so many Chinese women who felt forced to accept their lot, Ah Toy challenged both her cultural heritage and the laws of her new land. She ran successful brothels, among other businesses, and brought young Chinese girls into a life of prostitution and bondage.

There is little to admire about Ah Toy. In fighting for her own freedom, she became as cruel as her oppressors. Exploitation, it seemed, made her feel free and powerful, and rather than use that freedom to help her fellow Chinese "sisters," she joined in the brutality. She was greedy and ruthless. Besides running brothels, Ah Toy was heavily involved in the Chinese flesh trade, importing Chinese girls, mostly through deceptive means, into a life so unforgiving that it was rare a prostitute would reach the age of twenty-five. It was rumored, but never proven, that she was also involved in murder, bribery, and blackmail. She knew how to use men, enslave women, and manipulate the laws.

Histories of Chinese women are rare. Most of the records we have were written by missionaries and journalists. Missionary documents give us some insight but are typically very condescending and reveal the cultural prejudices many in the United States had about the Chinese. Well-meaning missionaries tried to rescue the non-Christian "Celestials"—the nineteenth-century American term for the Chinese or Chinese prostitutes—from their doom. Many diaries were diatribes, more sermon than history, showing a shallow understanding of the culture or the people.

Most journalists in the mid-nineteenth century were anything but objective. Their work tended to be ethnocentric. Racism was rampant in the West. Chinese emigrants were considered substandard human beings—having a weak character, utterly lacking in principle and virtue.

They were also thought to be sexually promiscuous, with no concept of family values. John Swinton, an influential lecturer and journalist for the *New York Sun*, wrote a pamphlet in 1870 titled "New Issue: The Chinese American Question." He argued that California needed to rid itself of the "Chinese menace." He suggested the Chinese were moral lightweights and more prone to disease—especially venereal disease—and would corrupt California. M. B. Starr wrote in his 1873 book *The Coming Struggle: Or, What the People of the Pacific Coast Think of the Coolie Invasion,* "[the Chinese] were heathen and Sodomites and San Francisco [was] a large bordello." An editorial from the *Tombstone Epitaph* in 1882 continued this line of attack:

> The Chinese are the least desired immigrants who have ever sought the United States. The most we can do is to insist that the heathen, a devourer of soup made of the fragrant juice of the rat, filthy, disagreeable, and undesirable generally, an encumbrance that we do not know how to get rid of, but whose tribe shall not increase in this part of the world.

As early as 1849, and with the financial backing of business owners in San Francisco, a hate group called the "Regulators" (also called the

"Hounds") took it upon themselves to do a bit of ethnic cleansing. They burned Chinese businesses and harassed, beat up, or killed Chinese men and women.

In his famous journals, miner Alfred Doten reflected his intolerance—and the intolerance of most frontiersmen—when he wrote about his mining camp being robbed. He automatically assumed the Chinese had robbed him. In a huff, he collected a bunch of mining buddies who were just as full of righteous indignation. He recorded: "We went and kicked up a row with the Chinese and told them we'd shoot them if they stole any more."

Against this cultural milieu and ethnic antipathy, Chinese men and women struggled to make a living in the American West, a supposed land of promise. By 1852, American miners had driven out almost 500 Chinese miners from claims at Yuba City, Columbia, and Mormon Bar.

Ah Toy's new home was nearly as punishing a place to live as her homeland. Ah Toy was born into a poor Chinese family near Canton. As a girl and young woman, her life in China was very difficult. Great Britain had won the Opium War, and China had been hit with years of famine. A female child was, at best, a burden, another mouth to feed. It was hoped that a family could marry off a daughter as soon as possible. If that wasn't possible, it wasn't unusual for a daughter to be sold to a marriage broker. A convoluted legal document was signed, and the girl was legally, but more importantly, morally, bound by family honor to do the broker's bidding. Although many girls were, indeed, married to countrymen, some of the less-than-honest brokers sent them to California to work as prostitutes.

Families might also indenture their daughters to another kind of broker who promised to take the girl to California, known as the Golden Mountain, where she would work off the price of the ocean voyage and expenses and then be married to a countryman. Often their contracts turned out to be far stricter than they'd imagined—contracts many unsuspecting girls would, unfortunately, never outlive. Some of these young women would become prostitutes on the San Francisco waterfront. During the Gold Rush, nearly every Chinese female in the city was employed in the sex trade.

As a young woman, Ah Toy likely found herself in a similar plight.

In 1848 or 1849, at the approximate age of twenty, Ah Toy was put on a boat to San Francisco, doomed to a life in the brothels; whether she was brokered or indentured is unknown. The conditions on the ships were horrific. A trip generally took from forty to sixty days, if the winds cooperated. People were packed like cordwood into the holds. The food was poor, and sometimes water was at a premium. Bunks were small and uncomfortable: six feet long, fifteen inches wide, with twenty to twenty-eight inches of headroom. On one such ship, the *Exchange*, 85 of the 613 Chinese passengers died. On the *Libertad*, more than 180 Chinese passengers died on the passage across the Pacific.

The foul living accommodations on a ship, however, were only the first of the horrors a young Chinese girl might experience. At sea, it was not uncommon to be raped by the crew members. Crews were encouraged by flesh brokers on both sides of the Pacific to "humble" or "break in" as many passengers as they could. Traders thought repeated rapes by crew members made their human cargo easier to deal with later on.

It didn't take long for the clever Ah Toy to compare her place in the hold with the captain's fine accommodations. And she saw the foul treatment the women received on the ship and wanted no part of it. Ah Toy was a beautiful woman, and she saw how the captain looked at her when she walked on deck. She played up to him, and in no time she had moved into his quarters and was enjoying all the amenities. Ah Toy reportedly left the ship in San Francisco with new silk robes and jewels. She had managed to escape the brutal treatment on the ship—and the ignominy of being sold on the Barracoon, the notorious auction block.

The Barracoon was in a rough part of San Francisco called Queens Row. A young woman on the block might sell for a few dollars or as much as several thousands of dollars. Because slavery, strictly speaking, was illegal, merchants and buyers got around the law by having the seller hand the girl the money, which she in turn handed back to the broker. Theoretically, she did this "freely" to prove that she was a "willing partner" in the deal. She also signed a contract stating that she had entered into this transaction of her own free will.

One might wonder why so few Chinese girls were able to escape their oppressors. After all, Ah Toy broke free of her chains and attained financial success and personal freedom. She was independent and liberated before it was fashionable, managing to recoil against her fat and the customs of her people—which is one reason why she stands out 150 years later. She was a maverick. Most women in her situation reluctantly accepted their fates. They came from a male-oriented culture where women were considered subservient, and daughters a burden. Most Chinese girls from an early age could recite the *Three Obediences* taught by Confucius: "When she is young, she obeys her father; when she is married, she obeys her husband; when she is widowed, she obeys her son." She knew that her duties were to be chaste, obedient, reticent, and pleasing. Even though prostitution might be distasteful and unchaste, her duty and honor to her family demanded fidelity to their wishes. She must comply if the dominant man in her life willed it—and that would also mean her broker.

If a young Chinese prostitute tried to escape, besides bringing dishonor to her family, she would be charged for the cost of her recapture. At one point, it was also possible for a runaway girl to be arrested for grand larceny; having "stolen" herself, she was in violation of California State Law. She would be charged and bail set. Her captors would then pay the bail, have the charges dropped, and get most of their money back; however, the full cost of the bail, along with the expenses involved with finding her, would increase the years on her contract.

If a girl (many were not in their teens yet) was attractive, she might become the mistress of a wealthy Chinese businessman or successful miner. After he was done with her services, she'd find herself in a higher-end brothel. As expected, the best-looking girls had an easier life. The rest of the "merchandise" was sold to common brothels or high-volume cribs, low-end brothels. The conditions of the cribs were particularly bad. A crib might be twelve by fourteen feet—where the girl would often ply her trade, sometimes until she died, committed suicide, or was sold. When a girl was no longer of use as a prostitute, she was sold to local farmers as an indentured field hand. One California doctor in the 1850s commented that he'd rarely seen a Chinese woman older than twenty, and at that age most looked like old women. He also commented that at least 90 percent of the crib girls had a venereal disease.

Many Chinese prostitutes, often just girls, spent their lives in small rooms called cribs.
Most died at an early age.

A red light district in San Francisco's Chinatown.

Not long after Ah Toy arrived in California, she decided to start her own business "entertaining" men—likely the first Chinese woman in the Gold Rush days to do so. She noticed men ogling her on the street, and she quickly realized that these love-starved miners would pay for a really good look at a Chinese woman if they had the opportunity. She rented a couple of rooms and hired carpenters to make the modifications she demanded: In one room, she had the carpenters build a platform for her striptease act. In the adjoining room, she bolted the door and had the carpenters drill peepholes so customers could watch as she undressed. Considering there were a lot of "lonesome" miners and very few women, she thought an ounce of gold would be a fair price for a glimpse of her naked. She hired a very large bouncer to collect the gold and keep freeloaders out. After the men paid the fee, she would walk on stage in her green silk pants and jacket. Her hair was perfect and her eyebrows plucked pencil thin. Men lined up around the block to see her perform. Ah Toy was the talk of the town. Time and time again, she did her act to the miners' cheers and whistles. She also made a great deal of money, and it was easier and safer than prostitution.

Apparently, though, some of the men watched her peep show so often they ran out of gold dust. Someone got the bright idea of passing off bronze shavings for gold. Her bouncer was big, but not very bright. Ah Toy was so mad she took the thieves to court in approximately 1853. She showed the judge the worthless shavings. She also told the court she was trying to better herself. Her case was dismissed because of her race, gender, and profession, but her pluck and ambition were noted, if not appreciated.

This incident sheds light on her character and drive. First, she had studied the English language and was comfortable enough to argue her case. Few Chinese women at this time attempted to master English. Second, for someone so new to California, she had developed a thorough understanding of the legal system. Most citizens had only a sketchy idea about how the legal system worked. Third, although she had low social status and few rights, she attempted to get legal redress for her griev-ances. More often than not, when a woman became a prostitute, she gave up her rights and protections under the law. Fourth, she was trying to compete with men on an equal footing. This act shows a lot of courage in a cultural milieu of prejudice and antipathy. She refused to be taken advantage of.

With money from her peep show, and with backing from some of her wealthy clients, Ah Toy expanded her business interests by opening an upscale brothel, which catered to more prosperous clientele. She had good business sense, and her brothel was a lucrative venture. In addition to the sex trade, she and her girls were always on the alert for important information that might prove useful in either blackmail or to other businessmen. She ventured into other "houses of sin," including high-volume brothels, and associated with some of the more powerful San Francisco businessmen.

As it would turn out, she was no stranger to the courtrooms. In 1853, the *Alta California* reported that the notorious Ah Toy was suing powerful local crime boss Yee Ah Tye, who had started to insist on taxing her a "protection fee," which she refused to pay. By filing a lawsuit and bringing her dispute out in the open, Ah Toy broke an unwritten code; Chinese business was Chinese business, and you didn't involve outsiders. People ended up floating in the San Francisco Bay for a lot less. Ah Toy won her suit against Yee Ah Tye and continued to do business as usual—without Yee Ah Tye's tax.

In 1854, laws were passed making it illegal for a Chinese person to testify against a Caucasian, and Ah Toy was no longer able to sue her Anglo clients. But this did not keep Ah Toy out of the courtroom. She was charged with running a "disorderly house," a house of prostitution. To fight the charges, she called upon some of her powerful friends who had become her silent business partners. They included judges, city officials, policemen, businessmen, and miners. They helped her run interference for her legal problems and would tip her off when raids and inspections were planned.

In addition to running her own houses, she found that the importation of girls was a lucrative business. Despite having seen the horrors firsthand on her own ocean voyage from China, Ah Toy began buying and selling Chinese women. She even supported the practice of crew members raping the young women aboard the ships to prepare them for their new profession. She was known to have the less cooperative girls transported in wooden or steel cages.

When laws were finally passed in 1870 making it a crime to forcibly bring women from China to the United States, Ah Toy got around the laws by proclaiming that the women she was dealing with were either married or espoused to Chinese men already in the country.

Ah Toy always found a way around the laws and never paid for her crimes. It is believed that she eventually handed over management of her businesses to a younger employee so she could retire in luxury. Because of the mythology that surrounds her, it is unknown if she stayed in the United States and enjoyed her ill-gotten prosperity or if she went back to China as a rich woman.

Eulogizing Ah Toy is difficult. In her struggle for independence, she became as corrupt, if not more so, than her own abusers. Her experiences did not make her more sensitive to the plights of her Chinese "sisters" or women in general, but, ironically, seemed to have left her more calloused. ⊷

BIBLIOGRAPHY

Adams, Andy. *The Log of a Cowboy: The Narrative of the Old Trail Days.* Boston: Houghton Mifflin, 2002.

Aldridge, Dorothy. *Historic Colorado City: The Town with a Future.* Colorado Springs: Little London Press, 1996.

Armitage, Susan, and Elizabeth Jameson, editor. *The Women's West.* Norman: University of Oklahoma Press, 1987.

Baker, Pearl. *Robbers Roost Recollections.* Logan: Utah State University Press, 1991.

———. *The Wild Bunch at Robbers Roost.* New York: Abelard-Schuman, 1971. Reprint, Lincoln: University of Nebraska Press, 1989.

Billington, Ray Allen. *America's Frontier Heritage.* New York: Holt, Rinehart and Winston, 1966.

Betenson, Bill. "Lula Parker Betenson." *The Outlaw Trail Journal,* Winter 1995.

Betenson, Lula, and Dora Flack. *Butch Cassidy, My Brother.* Provo, Utah: Brigham Young University Press, 1975.

Brown, Robert L. *Colorado Ghost Towns Past and Present.* Caldwell, Idaho: Caxton, 1981.

Buck, Daniel, and Anne Meadows. "Etta Place: A Most Wanted Woman." *The Journal of the Western Outlaw–Lawmen History Association*, vol. 3, no. 1, Spring–Summer 1993.

———. "Etta Place: Wild Bunch Mystery Lady." *The English Westerners' Society Tally Sheet*, Spring 1993.

Burton, Doris Karren. "Charley Crouse's Robbers' Roost." *The Outlaw Trail Journal*, Winter 1993.

Butler, Anne M., and Ona Siporin. *Uncommon Common Women: Ordinary Lives of the West*. Logan: Utah State University Press, 1996.

Dary, David. *Seeking Pleasure in the Old West*. Lawrence: University Press of Kansas. 1995.

Davidson, Art. *Sometimes Cassidy*. Salt Lake City: Hawkes Publishing, 1994.

DeJournette, Dick, and Dawn DeJournette. *One Hundred Years of Brown's Park and Diamond Mountain*. Cheyenne: Mansfield Printing, Inc., 1996.

Drago, Gail. *Etta Place: Her Life and Times with Butch Cassidy and the Sundance Kid*. Plano: Republic of Texas Press, 1996.

———. "Black Gold and the Wild Bunch." *Quarterly of the National Association and Center for Outlaw and Lawmen History*, March 1944.

Dullenty, Jim. *The Butch Cassidy Collection*. Hamilton, Montana: Rocky Mountain House Press, 1986.

———. "The Farm Boy Who Became a Member of Butch Cassidy's Wild Bunch." *Quarterly of the National Association and Center for Outlaw and Lawmen History*, Winter 1986.

————. "Friends of the Pinkertons." *Quarterly of the National Association and Center for Outlaw and Lawmen History,* June 1995.

————. *From Cowboy to Outlaw: The True Story of Will Carver.* Sonora, Texas: Sutton County Historical Society, 1995.

————. "The Sundance Kid: Wyoming Cowboy." *The Journal of Western Outlaw–Lawman Historical Association,* Spring 1992.

Goldman, Marion S. *Gold Diggers and Silver Miners: Prostitution and Social Life on the Comstock Lode.* Ann Arbor: University of Michigan Press, 1981.

Gould, Lewis. *Wyoming: A Political History, 1868–1896.* New Haven: Yale University Press, 1968.

Gray, Dorothy. *Women of the West.* Lincoln, Nebraska: Bison Books, 1998.

Gray, James H. *Red Lights on the Prairies.* New York: Signet, New American Library, 1971.

Hine, Robert V. *The American West: An Interpretive History.* Boston: Little Brown, 1973.

Horan, James. *Desperate Women.* New York: G. P. Putnam's Sons, 1952.

Hunter, J. Marvin, editor. *The Trail Drivers of Texas.* Nashville: Cokesbury Press, 1925.

Jones, James, Billy Jones, et al. *Women of Texas.* Waco: Texan Press, 1972.

Kessler-Harris, Alice. *Out to Work: A History of Wage-Earning Women in the United States.* New York: Oxford University Press, 1982.

Lamar, Howard R., editor. *The Reader's Encyclopedia of the American West.* New York: Thomas Y. Crowell, 1977.

Lee, Bob, editor. *Gold Gals, Guns, Guts: A History of Deadwood, Lead, and Spearfish, 1874–1976.* Pierre: South Dakota State Historical Society Press, 2004.

McLoughlin, Denis. *Wild and Woolly: An Encyclopedia of the Wild West.* New York: Barnes and Noble, Inc., 1975.

Meadows, Anne. *Digging Up Butch and Sundance.* New York: St. Martin's Press, 1994.

Miller, Stuart Creighton. *The Unwelcome Immigrant: The American Image of the Chinese, 1784–1882.* Berkeley: University of California Press, 1969.

Morn, Frank. *The Eye that Never Sleeps: A History of the Pinkerton National Detective Agency.* Bloomington: Indiana University Press, 1982.

O'Neal, Bill. *Encyclopedia of Western Gunfighters.* Norman: University of Oklahoma Press, 1979.

Reiter, Joan Swallow. *The Old West: The Women.* Alexandria, Virginia: Time Life Books, 1978.

Riley, Glenda. *The Female Frontier: A Comparative View of Women on the Prairie and the Plains.* Lawrence: University Press of Kansas, 1988.

Riley, Glenda, and Richard W. Etulain, editors. *Wild Women of the Old West.* Golden, Colorado: Fulcrum Publishing, 2003.

Rosa, Joseph G. *The Gunfighter: Man or Myth?* Norman: University of Oklahoma Press, 1969.

———. *They Called Him Wild Bill: The Life and Adventures of James Butler Hickok.* Norman: University of Oklahoma Press, 1974.

Rutter, Michael. *Myths and Mysteries of the Old West.* Guilford, Connecticut: Twodot, 2005.

————. *Outlaw Tales of Utah*. Guilford, Connecticut: Twodot, 2003.

————. *Upstairs Girls*. Helena, Montana: Farcountry Press, 2005.

————. *Wild Bunch Women*. Guilford, Connecticut: Twodot, 2003.

Selcer, Richard F. *Hell's Half Acre*. Fort Worth: Texas Christian University Press, 1991.

Snell, Joseph. *Painted Ladies of the Cowtown Frontier*. Kansas City: Kansas City Posse of the Westerners, 1965.

West, Elliot. *The Saloon on the Rocky Mountain Mining Frontier*. Lincoln: University of Nebraska Press, 1979.

Williams, George, III. *The Red-Light Ladies of Virginia City, Nevada*. Carson City: Tree by the River Publishing, 1984.

Wilson, John P. *Merchants, Guns and Money: The Story of Lincoln County and its Wars*. Santa Fe: Museum of New Mexico Press, 1987.

Wright, Robert. *Dodge City, The Cowboy Capital*. Wichita: Robert Wright, 1913.

INDEX

Michael Rutter has authored or co-authored nearly 40 books and 600 articles for magazines and newspapers. He is a passionate historian and outdoorsman—and a fanatic fly fisherman.

He was awarded the Ben Franklin Award for Outdoor Writing and the Rocky Mountain Book Publishers Association Award. Michael teaches advanced writing at Brigham Young University. He is also a Christa McAuliffe Fellow.

Michael Rutter lives in Orem, Utah, with his wife, Shari. They have two charming children, two spoiled cats, and a yellow Lab named Peabody.